The Art and Science of

Public Speaking

Swapnil Saurav

The Art and Science of Public Speaking

If you've been asked to give a public speech, you may wonder: what is public speaking and why is public speaking important? Those questions are quite logical if you've never thought much about public speaking before.

Because public speaking is done before a live audience, there are some special factors the speaker needs to take into consideration.

In this book, we'll define public speaking for you. We will connect you to some resources that can help you become a better public speaker including some public speaking examples. Whether you're a small business owner, a student, or just someone who's passionate about something—you'll benefit. It:

- Improves confidence
- Better research skills
- Stronger deductive skills
- Ability to advocate for causes
- And more

Happy Learning!

Series: Boost your career
Author: Swapnil Saurav
ISBN: 978-81-946334-3-3
Review/Feedback: ekapresshyderabad@gmail.com
Website: www.ekapress.org

When we fear public speaking or are required to give a speech you may ask yourself why is public speaking important? Believe it or not but public speaking is one of the most important skills you will ever develop in your life.

Public speaking is so important that it could be the deciding factor in many things such as your career development, your business growth and even in the relationships you have with your friends and family. Throughout history it has been public speaking that has united people and caused great change, both positive and negative. Public speaking is important, both in history and in your life.

Public speaking is important because it increases your skills at speaking (an activity we do every single day) and thus even when you are with one other person, as opposed to a group, you are less likely to be awkward and more likely to be comfortable and confident.

90% of people will avoid getting up in front of people to give a speech. By standing up and speaking to a crowd you are positioning yourself as an expert in your field and you have a great opportunity to share your knowledge. People follow leaders who inspire them and leaders who communicate their ideas effectively. If you can't communicate with your tribe you can't be a leader.

I think I have given your enough reason to read this book ☺ I have covered every aspect of public speaking in this book. Learn and Master this important skill.

SWAPNIL SAURAV

ABOUT THE AUTHOR

Swapnil Saurav

Swapnil Saurav is a Coach and Speaker. He makes his living by working in Software Industry. He has over 17 years of work experience in IT industry with focus on Supply Chain Analytics.

He has been invited to be the key note speaker at various industry forums and has a passion for teaching & developing leaders for tomorrow.

Swapnil's expertise lies in figuring out ways to do what others say can't be done. He holds MBA from S.P. Jain Institute of Management & Research, M.S. (BITS, Pilani) and B.E. (Visvesvaraya Technological University).

Website: www.swapnil.asia

Linked In profile: https://in.linkedin.com/in/swapnilsaurav

Contents

UNIT 1: Public Speaking for Beginners

Chapter 1: Identify the purpose

Speaking in front of people, large crowds in particular, is usually perceived as the most stressful experience imaginable. The following ideas in this course are designed to help you, or *anyone* for that matter, convey your ideas and messages to either one person, or a large group in just about *any* setting. Creating an effective presentation, can seem very overwhelming. But here are strategies you can use to come up with an effective and powerful speech in 30 minutes or less, regardless of your target audience.

#1 Identifying your purpose

#1 Identifying your purpose

- Begin with the end in mind

- The essence of public speaking is not to GAIN but to GIVE

- What is the 'call to action' for your speech?

The importance of goal-setting must not be overlooked when preparing for any presentation. The very first thing you need do before you even embark on your presentation is to define your objectives. It is crucial that you begin with the end in mind. Ask yourself this, "What do I want to achieve from my speech?", "What do I want my audience to receive?", "What do I want my audience to do next?"

The first thing you need to do in the speech preparation process is to identify your purpose. The purpose of your presentation can range from creating awareness, fostering understanding, generating impact, selling a product, or even to inspire your audience. Remember that the main reason why you're presenting in the first place is to give, not just gain. As such, your goals should be aligned with allowing your audience to benefit from your presentation. Your purpose-setting must be extremely clear, not just to yourself, but to your audience as well. This helps them internally craft the benefits they will gain from listening to you.

The biggest mistake of public speaking is when you start with the wrong purpose in mind. Mediocre speakers operate without a specific purpose which can easily cause stress and anxiety. The nature of your purpose is *just as important* as the purpose itself. Many speakers often mistakenly assume or even subconsciously decide that their purpose is audience validation and approval. Wrong. This is completely foolish. This causes great pressure on the speaker to be absolutely perfect in order to win unanimous approval and this causes a great deal of anxiety. I call this a "stress-producing" purpose.

Once you've established the purpose of your presentation, you can easily craft your presentation around it in order for it to be achieved. Remember that the essence of public speaking is not to GAIN something, but to GIVE something. When you operate with that frame of mind, you automatically tune your body language, tone of voice and craft content that is useful for your audience. With that, you immediately attract the attention of the majority.

To conclude this section, here's a quick summary. Before even writing your speech, you need to clearly define your objectives and ask yourself, "What do you want to achieve with this?" and to set goals that benefit not just yourself, but your audience as well. Now that you've identified the purpose of your speech, you can move on to the next stage.

#2 Preparing your speech

#2 Preparing your speech

- Does the speech pass the 'business card' test?

- Draft your speech with 4-5 key points

Now that you've identified the *purpose* of your speech, it's time you craft it. But before you do, it's important to clarify your topic. One way to make sure you've got it all cleared up is to try out the "business card test" - can you state your main idea on only *one* side of a business card? If you can, you're ready to move on. If you can't, keep working on it until you can.

Now, you can start drafting your speech. Grab a sheet of paper and right at the top of the page, clearly state your desired topic and the goal of your presentation. Then move on to write your opening lines and follow that up with 4-5 key points. Back these points up and summarize them in the conclusion. This is your outline. Now that you've listed your most important subjects, you can begin crafting your presentation based on the completed outline.

Before you start writing that speech out proper, let's take a quick detour, and visit one of the greatest and most notable speeches made in human history - yes, Martin Luther King, Jr.'s "I Have A Dream". Did you know that the most important, most often-quoted and the most powerful part of his entire speech, his iconic "I have a dream" statement, was made only in the last quarter of his entire powerful presentation? It makes you wonder how he managed to capture the full attention of over 200, 000 agitated, and angry civil rights supporters? If you were thinking that it was his authority, you're wrong. And it wasn't his looks either. Reverend King had a powerful introduction. He started with this, *"Five score years ago, a great American, in whose symbolic shadow we stand today, signed the Emancipation Proclamation. This momentous decree came as a great beacon light of hope to millions of Negro slaves who had been seared in the flames of withering injustice. It came as a joyous daybreak to end the long night of their captivity."*

Martin Luther King, Jr. started his powerful speech with a strong, passionate story which set the mood for the rest of his speech. When you begin crafting your speech, you have to remember that the most important part is your introduction. If your audience's attention is not captured within the first 30 seconds, you're pretty much history. Your introduction can make, or break, your entire speech. Remember that a strong opening is King, pun unintended. You may start with a probing question, a strong statement, a personal story or even a quote. These elements not only set the mood for your speech, but also pique your audience's attention and focus sufficiently to hook them for the rest of what you have to say.

Now that you've crafted a powerful introduction, you can move on to the core points of your speech. Each of these points should be backed by interesting stories, illustrations, historical references, humorous anecdotes, and examples that the audience may be able to relate to. Common stories or illustrations include references to common childhood occurrences, growing up pains or even teenage experiences. You can use these stories and examples to further reinforce your point. Humans are sensory creatures. If you're able to pique more than just one sense - their hearing - you've got them hooked, forever. Remember to include descriptives in your stories and even images for the visual ones in your audience. Analogies help your audience connect the dots of your points in their heads. Also remember to open and close each point with a clear transition. This makes it easier for your audience to follow your story. For those of you who're selling to or motivating your audience, you may even address your audience's pain, stress on the benefits of taking immediate actions, suggest a recommended course of action followed by closing remarks.

Now that you've detailed all the main points of your speech, you can start to write your close. A common, but effective, conclusion is a summary. This can be followed by an appeal or a call to action to challenge your audience, which is completely dependent on your purpose and topic. Run a quick summary by your audience and if necessary, outline clear guidelines and next actions they can take with the information you've just given them so that they do not feel like they've left your speech with nothing concrete to take with them.

#2 Preparing your speech

- Identify your purpose
- Clarify your topic
- Draft your speech
- Craft your introduction
- List the main points you wish to convey
- Write your close and end your speech

Here's a quick summary of the preparation process: 1. Identify your purpose, 2. Clarify your topic, 3. Draft your speech, 4. Craft your introduction, 5. List the main points you wish to convey, and 6. Write your close and end your speech with clear step-by-step or listed guides or next actions for your audience.

Let's move on to the next part of this session.

#3 Preparing your visual aids

- Flip charts
- Font
- Colors
- K.I.S.S.
- Less is more

In Martin Luther King, Jr.'s time, visual aids weren't just a luxury - they were an hassle, and in some cases, an impossibility. Thanks to technological advances today, you have projectors in almost every main hall of a speaking event, or a *white board* with markers at the very least. As such, it's no excuse to *not* have visual aids accompanying your speech.

Why are visual aids so important? They stimulate another one of your audience's senses and forces their brain to link the two together. This inadvertently helps keep them awake and focused throughout your speech. Most importantly, they allow you to further reinforce your points to your audience, and increase the number of associations their brain makes which can heighten your audience's recall of your topic. Let me share with you two very commonly used, and highly effective, visual aids that will captivate your audience's attention and help cue you as your speak.

Firstly, flip charts. Flip charts are huge pads of paper that are mounted on a portable easel. This visual aid is best used with a relatively small audience - typically 20 or fewer - unless there's a camera to magnify the chart for the rest of the hall. You can use bold or dark colors against a white flip chart to increase the ease of reading. A flip chart can be prepared *prior* to your presentation, but the power of the flip chart is that it can be used for drawing or writing *during* your presentation. Many motivational speakers adopt the flip chart, why? Because in comparison with powerpoint presentations, a flip chart allows the presenter to have a wider range of body movement in order to reinforce and reiterate their points with gestures and force.

Next up, you've got the powerpoint presentation. These days using a laptop, a projector and Microsoft PowerPoint or the Apple Keynote program is the norm. Technological advances have allowed us to produce dramatic, high-resolution visual aids such as animation and simulations. Today, computer-based visual aids are becoming the standard for many technical, educational and even business-related presentations. The power of the powerpoint presentation is that it can be used for both small and large audiences and can convey both simple and highly complex information. Today, with remote control devices, you can even change your visuals as you walk about the stage. If you've ever watched TED videos online, or attended a TED Talk, you'll know what I mean. The challenge with computer-based visuals is that you need to keep them simple. There are *many* things to consider when crafting your presentation. Here are a few you can keep in mind.

Firstly, your font. Not only is font-size important, your *choice* of font affects readability significantly. Always stick to high readability fonts such as "Times New Roman", "Arial" or "Helvetica". San-serif fonts are preferred as they usually increase readability. If these fonts seem "boring" or "distasteful" to you, scrap that thought. Your audience will thank you profusely for using these fonts.

Secondly, your colors. Choose colors that heighten readability. Remember that red text against a black background is a terror to read, and the same for vice-versa. Stick to pale, pastel backgrounds and dark text color such as black, or dark, black/brown backgrounds and white text color. And remember that your text should only have a maximum of three colors. If you fear that your presentation has become too monotone, you can always opt for colorful images and pictures to add a splash of life to your slideshow. But remember to choose your pictures wisely and to not let them upstage you and your speech.

Thirdly, K.I.S.S. Yes, keep it simple and suggestive. I'm talking about the text. It's a presentation faux pas to *read your slides* to your audience. You should know everything inside out and only occasionally turn to your slides for a cue or reference. Most importantly, the main points of your presentation should *not* be in your visual aids. The text in your visual aids should only allude to your main points. Use bullet points instead of full sentences in order to decrease the wordiness of your visual aid. This also applies for your charts and diagrams. Don't present them a full-fledged chart with 20 components to decipher. If your presentation requires charts and graphs, slice the data for your audience beforehand. They don't need to know *everything* - only your key findings and the significant statistics.

Lastly, less is more. This is in reference to your animation. You can use animation to reiterate a point, or even create some drama and suspense. But to animate *every single word* or object in your presentation is a *huge* no-no. Not only will you heavily distract your audience, you may also give them a headache.

To quickly summarize, flip charts are great to use with smaller crowds and give you wider range of movement. If you're considering using powerpoint or keynote slides as a visual aid, remember the 4 rules to increase readability and audience attention: 1. Simple font, 2. High contrast and minimal colors, 3. Keep it simple and suggestive, and 4. less animation is more.

Visual aids are huge help for presentations and should be used if possible. However, avoid the number one mistake made by many novice speakers: Do not let your visual aids control you. You control the presentation. Your visual aid, is merely an "aid" and is not the entire show. Use it to reiterate and back up your points and don't make it the point of the *entire* presentation. Remember that the point of your visual aid is to motivate your audience and arouse their imagination to help them to empathize with your idea and topic and visualize it far beyond what is visible in the ephemeral PowerPoint slide they currently view.

Now that you've got speech and presentation basics covered, let's move on to something a little bit more practiced.

#4 Creating a mock presentation

#4 Creating a mock presentation

- Smile and speak aloud

- Record your rehearsal

- **Pay attention to body language!**

The one way to eliminate stress and fear before your presentation day is to rehearse. Consistent practice will not only significantly boost your confidence, but it will also help you remember and become more accustomed to your material. Let me run through with you the basic structure of a rehearsal.

First, memorize your opening sentence. This is crucial as once you've got into the beat of things, you'll realize that the rest flows in more smoothly. Next, memorize your main points in order of your presentations. Try to come up with acronyms for your points and run them in your head consistently while preparing. Also, remember your transitions. In between each point, remember your choice of transition into the next point. Relate your transition sentence to your main point and you will easily recall it during your actual presentation. Lastly, remember your stories. The best way to do so is not to create stories, but to use actual personal experiences. This way you won't have to try to hard to memorize details and feelings, but the story itself will come naturally to you and even if you forget the flow of the story, you'll have your memory to help you.

While practicing, it's important to smile and speak aloud, even if you're alone. Believe me when I say that presenting in your head is not the same as speaking it aloud. Simulating an actual presentation even when alone can help you build confidence and help you create the atmosphere of an actual presentation. When I say simulate - I mean go all out. Smile, use gestures, refer to your visual aids, practice your posture - all this may seem silly, but it really helps increase your energy and enthusiasm, indirectly injecting this same energy into your audience on the real day.

When you simulate your presentation to an actual audience, start by getting your friends and family to help you out. If you get nervous when speaking to a large audience. Start small. Start out practicing to an audience of 2 - your parents or siblings perhaps. Gather their feedback and move on to a larger practice group of 4. Ask your friends for a hand and get them to sit in and provide you with their honest opinions. Then move on a practice group of 8, and repeat this process to a larger group of friends. Remember to obtain feedback from every group and reflect on your flaws and the specific things that you can improve on. Remember to ask your audience to be critical and nitpick on all your presentation flaws. You want to be able to learn from your mistakes, big or small, before the real thing.

Another important thing to do is to record your rehearsal. Record it in video format if you can. Why do I suggest recording? This is so you can reflect on your own presentation aside from your audience. Put yourself in the shoes of a viewer or listener and identify your mistakes or less glorious moments. Focus your attention on the pacing and timing of your speech as well and take notes for your following practice.

Lastly, your body language is particularly important as they send subliminal messages to your audience. Walk straight and tall, make constant and firm eye contact with your audience, smile constantly and use gestures to help inject some versatility and movement into your presentation. Not only will this convey a less wooden message to your audience, this can also help to dissipate nervous tension.

To quickly summarize - practice, reflect, practice. That's the key to presentation success. Rehearse to small groups, slowly increase the headcount in those groups and obtain feedback from your mock audience. Record your rehearsals and analyze your own speech and presentation style and place particular emphasis on your body language.

Chapter 2: Eliminate Stage Fright

#1 Eliminate stage fright and build your self confidence

- Fear is **not** pain, but the mere **anticipation** of it

- 5 causal elements of stage fright: imagination of people judge, possibility of failure, inherent need to do well, feeling of uncertainty, excessive focus on one's own behavior and appearance

#1 Eliminate stage fright and build your self confidence

Are you the type who cringes at the *thought* of walking on stage? The type that is overcome by sweaty palms, a racing heartbeat and shaky legs the moment you take your first step on that platform. If you are, don't think of yourself any less. Fear of public speaking is highly common and almost everyone has experienced or felt it at one point in their lives. In fact, statistics show that some degree of public speaking fear/nervousness affects an estimated 95% of all speakers. In fact, recent studies in the United States of America have shown that fear of public speaking actually ranks higher than fear of death! Don't you find it bizarre that the general American public fear facing crowds more than the prospect of Heaven or Hell?

That being said - let's dissect this common feeling in order to understand it better. Let's start with what is fear? Fear is defined as the anticipation of pain. Yes, you heard that right. Fear is not pain, but the mere anticipation of it. There are 5 causal elements of stage fright: 1. The perception or imagination of the presence of people who will judge, 2. The possibility of failure, 3. The inherent need to do well in order to avoid failure, 4. The feeling of uncertainty of whether one can do well and 5. An excessive focus on one's own behavior and appearance.

The reason why we experience uncomfortable symptoms like light-headedness, sweaty palms, and increased heart rate is because this fear is actually a psychological condition that is manifested physically via these symptoms! So in order to prevent these symptoms, we have to conquer fear. How do we do this? By attacking every one of the 5 causal symptoms. In this session I'll reveal 6 very simple steps to help you overcome your fear of speaking to audiences on stage.

#1 Eliminate stage fright and build your self confidence

- **Step 1: Be audience-centered**
- **Step 2: Accept that you make mistakes**
- **Step 3: Ditch all that negative self-talk**
- **Step 4: Convert your fear into positive energy**
- **Step 5: Present daily**
- **Step 6: Practice Makes Near Perfect**

Step 1: Be audience-centered.

In order to conquer fear, you have to remember that your presentation is not about yourself. Instead, it's really about your audience. Focus on the needs of your audience, rather than on how you will perform and your fears will automatically disappear. The truth is, no one really cares about your voice, or how you look. Your audience is more interested in what you have to offer them. Concentrate on how you can provide optimum benefit to the people listening to you. If you're selling a product, concentrate your efforts on selling the benefits of your product to your audience. If you're sharing a learning, focus on how they can benefit or take action with what you have to share. Whether or not you are telling a story to build rapport, or delivering a sales pitch, a focus on your audience's needs can help take your mind off your fear.

Step 2: Accept that you make mistakes

No one is born a perfect speaker. Good public speakers aren't born, they're made. Do you think Martin Luther King, Jr. delivered that amazing speech on his first try? That man was a Reverend who had delivered countless speeches and sermons prior to "I Have A Dream". Even he made mistakes. So if you screw up, does it *really* matter? What's most important is that you learn from your mistakes. If you notice a mistake during your speech, no one in the audience is going to disapprove if you backtrack to amend that mistake. In fact, it's more credible that you do. In order to improve and be better, you have to take risks. Think of your presentation as an opportunity to benefit and convey amazing information to your audience. And remember this, Thomas Edison failed thousands of times before he invented the light bulb. And did it deter him? No. His inventions are spread across the world today and are constantly innovated upon. Do you want to be a Thomas Edison, or the chump who's too afraid to leave his house for fear he falls?

Step 3: Ditch all that negative self-talk

If you remember the causal elements of stage fright I just mentioned, you'll notice that all of those elements have a recurring theme - negative self-talk. Just like how the seeds of a tree determine its fruits or end product, what happens on the inside has a significant impact on our outside. This means that our actions and fears are actually influenced by our subconscious minds Negative self-talk not only drains your energy, it demotivates you. In order to overcome this, you need to start replacing all that negative self-talk with positive ones. Stand in front of the mirror daily, straight-backed and with a smile on your face. Replace your "I can't do this", "People will judge me" and "I'm going to suck" thoughts with phrases like "I feel energetic!", "I'm prepared and focused!", "I am delivering value to my audience!" and "The audience is my friend, not foe." Eventually, the attitude and actions will follow. Like the famous saying goes, you've got to fake it till you make it.

Step 4: Convert your fear into positive energy.

Did you know that aside from your thoughts, you can also convert your physical behavior? You can help convert stage fright symptoms with the power of visualization and belief. For example, did you know that sweaty palms and a racing pulse are also symptoms of an adrenaline rush? So instead of attributing negative thoughts to your racing pulse and sweaty palms, why don't you decipher these physical reactions as an adrenaline rush? As excitement and optimism for your presentation? This not only decreases your fear, it also immediately turns on the alertness and energy switch in your body. Your physical reactions are what you make them to be.

Aside from that, if you find yourself blanking out midway through your presentation, don't panic. You can choose one of two routes. You can either be honest, tell your audience you forgot and need to refer to your notes and laugh it off with a joke on aging, or you can side track a little and tell your audience a story of a funny thing that happened to you recently. Both routes give you a minute to realign your thoughts, give the audience a minute to laugh and humanize you to your audience.

If dry throat is your stage fright symptom, tell the organizers beforehand to prepare a glass of warm water or tea (cold drinks constrict your throat and cause more discomfort than comfort) and take an occasional sip in between your points. This not only gives your audience a minute to take notes, you are also offered a moment to recoup your thoughts and ready yourself for your next section. Remember to only take a sip though, and not gulp the entire glass down.

Step 5: Present daily

I'm not just talking about practice (I'll get into that later), I'm talking about incorporating it into your daily life. To tell you the truth, speaking to an audience is no different from your day-to-day interaction with the people around you. In a conversation, you're either trying to convey a message or sell an idea - both require the same skills and elements in a public presentation. Once you grasp and understand this concept, this can help you feel much more confident and powerful on stage. When you're talking to your friends, try to visualize yourself on a stage and imagine that they are your audience - how they react to you in that scenario is really how they will react to you on stage, with the exception that your friends can actually interrupt you. One way of gaining confidence and overcoming fear, is to incorporate elements of your public speaking skills into your daily conversations with your boss, colleagues, friends and family. Take careful notice of how they respond and you can easily tweak your conversation style to produce your desired reactions.

Step 6: Practice Makes Near Perfect.

I'm repeating this point from our last session because it is that important. This may seem simple enough, but the truth is the more you know your material, the more confident you'll be as the fear of forgetting will disappear almost entirely. Like I mentioned previously, practice your speech on 2 people, then 4, 8 and so on. Carefully assess your feelings whether it's confidence or anxiety throughout the presentation and record your practice groups' feedback. Again, remember that it doesn't have to be perfect and instead will get better as you go along and practice more. With time and sufficient practice, your presentation skills will drastically improve to the extent where you no longer have to worry about embarrassing yourself or screwing up.

Before we move on to the next point, let me quickly summarize the 6 steps to help overcome stage fright: 1. Be audience-centered, 2. Accept that you can make mistakes, 3. Ditch your negative self-talk, 4. Convert your fear into positive energy, 5. Present daily, and 6. Practice makes near perfect.

Now that you've got the basics of presentation preparation and the steps to eliminate stage fright down to a T, let's move on to personalizing your presentation.

#2 Incorporating your personality into your presentation

- Integrate personal stories

- Illustrate your physical style

- Keep your jewelry to a minimum

- Humor injects personality into your speech

One common trait among great presenters is that they have a distinct style which makes your speech memorable and helps inject *your* personality into your presentation. This helps keep your audience excited. Obama often incorporates slogans and refrains in his speeches, and Steve Jobs is a visual-zen master who designs strategic placements of empty slides in order to make his images stronger, and more prominent when they appear. Like Obama and Steve Jobs, you need to allocate time to focus on conveying your style in the most exciting manner possible.

One way to incorporate your personality is to integrate personal stories in your speech. This is not only an effective way of exposing your audience to who you are, it also helps them relate with you at a more emotional and personal level. One kind of personal story that usually does the trick is the success / hero story. You can speak of yourself as someone who overcame a huge obstacle in life that is relevant to your topic of presentation. This not only allows the audience to relate, sympathize and empathize with you, but also adds some credibility and authority to what you are about to share with them.

Another way of embodying your personality in your presentation is to illustrate your physical style. In other words, by how you dress. It's important to look the part of the message you're trying to convey. Top Internet marketer, Frank Kern's, selling point is freedom. This is why whenever he speaks to audiences, he's in surf shorts, a loose t-shirt with his hair in a wild disarray - he's subliminally conveying the message of freedom to his audience. That being said, there are a few guidelines you should take into account when deciding what to wear on stage.

Firstly, keep your jewelry to a minimum. Adorning yourself with too much "bling" can distract your audience from your speech and the only thing they'll take back with them at the end of your presentation will be how bright and shiny you were. Secondly, stay away from overly colorful articles of clothing. A pair of pants with stripes in 5 contrasting colors will only remind them of a clown from their childhood, and not a person of authority. That being said, overly monotonous clothing may help blend you into the background, making you irrelevant and completely unmemorable to your audience. Your clothing should only *reiterate* your point, not run the show. Always remember that the audience's main focus should be on what you have to share with them, and nothing else.

Humor is another great way to inject some personality into your presentation. Not only can it help grasp your audience's attention, it can also liven up the atmosphere. However, if you choose to use humor in the presentation, make sure your jokes are original, and not cliche. Try not to make fun of members of your audience and instead turn the joke on yourself. For example, if you are a person of short stature, you may want to poke fun at your height to illustrate a point that is relevant to your speech. If you notice that your jokes are falling flat on the audience, don't be dejected. Punctuate them with short, nonchalant quips such as "Damn, I'll remember to keep that to myself the next time." or even "Crap, my mom thought it was funny. I'll remember not to ask for her advice on humor next time".

At the end of the day, incorporating personality basically means be yourself. Your audience may not be psychic, but they will be able to see through a false persona. Therefore there is no better physical presentation than your genuine self. So relax, loosen up, and remind yourself to have a great time. A relaxed presenter who's enjoying his or herself automatically opens up the audience and loosens them up. Your audience is a mirror of who you project yourself to be.

#3 Extra stuff you need to help you convey a high-impact message

#3 Extra stuff you need to help you convey a high-impact message

- Platform skills

- Allow a wide range of pitches and tones

- Your body language and gestures

- Invoke **attention, interest and emotion**

Let me share with you some extra elements you can add to give your presentation that extra "zing" it needs to go from good to great.

Platform skills play a pretty crucial role in getting your audience to not just pay attention to you but to also get them excited and enthusiastic about your message. The pacing of your presentation, the pitch, tone and volume of your voice and even your vocal variety play important roles in helping you convey your message effectively. These tools help you clarify and support your message, emphasize your ideas, and even dramatize your message. Consistently maintaining a high volume and loud tone of voice will make you come across as excessively authoritative or aggressive, while using low volumes and soft tones may make you come across as too timid and decrease your credibility as a speaker and the lack of variation will make you sound too monotonous.

The best and most effective route is to allow yourself a wide range of pitches and tones. Adding variety to your vocal pattern is a surefire way to engage your audience's attention and reinforce key ideas to them. In addition to that, a well-timed moment of silence or pause can help you further emphasize certain ideas, or in some situations, dramatize your message with a little suspense or anticipation. Some good uses of pauses include pausing after you tell a joke to provide emphasis, and give your audience a moment to quieten their laughter. Another good use of the pause is right after you're introduced to your audience as it gives them time to refocus their attention on the presentation.

Aside from your tone of voice, your body language and gestures are also important components in relaying a more meaningful and memorable speech by adding punctuation. Did you know that the human body contains more than 700 muscles?

It's sad to know that only a handful of those muscles are used by speakers. Speakers tend to focus most of their attention in the search of the perfect words and the most precious points, thereby forgetting that our bodies speak louder than words ever could. When I say body language, I don't mean using your arms and fingers in a death grip clutch on a poor lectern, or frenetically clicking on your PowerPoint slides - I mean allowing your body to move naturally.

While a good message is important in a presentation, your effectiveness as speaker is really about your ability to invoke attention, interest and emotion in your audience through non-verbal communication. An amazing message conveyed with terrible body language does *not* get the point across. Why is that? Because your listeners don't only judge you and your message based on what they hear - they also take in to consideration what they *see*.

How to incorporate good body language

- Maintaining eye contact with your audience (3-5 seconds)

- 'Plant' a listener to watch out for distracting mannerisms

- Allow your body to move naturally

- Lastly, remember to smile!

When speaking to an audience, your body can be used as a very effective tool for adding emphasis and clarity to your words. It also plays a very important role in convincing your audience of your sincere feelings, your earnestness in educating or sharing with them, and your enthusiasm about your topic. No matter the purpose of your speech, the exterior self that you project must be appropriate and relevant to what you say.

Here are a few ways you can incorporate good body language into your presentations. Firstly, you can start with maintaining eye contact with your audience. You should not just continuously pass your gaze throughout the room, instead, try focusing your sight on individual members of the audience. You'll find that you can create a bond with them *just* by looking them directly in the eyes for 3-5 seconds. By using eye contact, you make everyone in your audience feel involved and connected to you.

Secondly, while in a practice session have a listener watch out for distracting mannerisms such as fidgeting, twitching, lip-biting, or key jingling. All these traits distract your audience from the key point of the message and focuses their attention on your nervousness and fear. You then immediately discredit yourself of any authority that you have on what you're talking about. You automatically seem unsure, and decrease the amount of trust your audience has about your message.

Thirdly, allow your body to move naturally by moving from one spot of the stage or platform to another. A good example is to walk to the other side of the stage as you move on to your next point, or move toward the audience when you ask a question. These subtle moves help your audience subconsciously visualize your transition from a point to another and help emphasize certain topics.

Lastly, remember to smile and actually express your emotions with your face. A smile can go a long way in helping the audience open up to you. That being said, constantly smiling throughout the entire speech only makes you look clinically insane. A variety of facial expressions that are relevant to what you're speaking about at the time can help you further punctuate your message. Surprise, curiosity, sadness, anger - these are but a handful of emotions that you can use while telling your audience a story in order for them to properly visualize it.

In summary, platform skills and effective use of body language can help you further punctuate your message and deliver a killer presentation. The keys to using them wisely? Variety and relevance. Always vary your tone of voice and body movements and always use them with relevance to whatever you're saying at the time.

Chapter 3: Know Your Audience

#1 Surveying the audience

- Speak to them personally before speech

- Look around to decipher the general age-group

- Ascertain if your cultural references are relevant

- Quickly assess their careers and stages of life.

Now that we've covered crafting your presentation, personalizing it and making it extraordinary, we can move on to more advanced stuff. In this session, we'll talk about ways to help you deal with an audience you've never met before and how to connect with them. In addition to that, we'll also cover the important, and often nerve-wrecking Q&A session that normally follows a presentation.

#1 Surveying the audience

Another core component of a killer presentation is audience interaction. The final part of any presentation - answering questions from the audience - can help you build trust and further establish your credibility as an expert on your subject. The thing is, this part of the presentation is the one part where you have close to no control over. Therefore the first step to succeeding in this arena is to getting to know your audience better.

Prior to your presentation, you should do a quick survey of your audience. There are a few ways you can do this and these methods are completely dependent on the nature of your presentation. If you're one of several speakers presenting to a large crowd of people, you may want to take a few minutes to mingle with your audience *before* your speech. Speak to them, look around to decipher the general age-group, ascertain if your cultural references are relevant and quickly assess their careers and stages of life. However, if you're speaking to board of directors of a large organization or several organizations, you may not have the luxury of mingling casually before you present. In that situation, you may want to do a quick background research of these specific individuals and their respective company profiles. If you're unable to do both, you can easily ask the organizer for the expected or targeted audience profile and work from there.

Here's why you should go through all this trouble and why it'll be worth it. By being aware of the characteristics and demographics of the people you speak to, you will be able to effectively tailor your presentation and pick your supporting points, anecdotes or analogies in order to reiterate what you need to say. Speaking to a group of 15-year-old students, for example, is very different from speaking to a group of 19-year-old students... much less an audience of professionals.

You'll find that audience-surveying is especially important when you're doing a technical presentation. In situations like that, you'll find that you need to assess your audience's level of awareness before you even craft your presentation so as to not bore or overwhelm them. Great public speakers understand that mistakes can always be overcome with connection, and information are greater shared with connection. If your audience is connected to you, you're less worried about forgetting a point, making an awkward statement or even looking slightly disheveled. You're less anxious about what ifs such as "what if I fall?" "what if the projector breaks down and my slides are gone forever?" or "what if I fart on stage?". With a connection, you're automatically less worried as all will be forgiven.

#2 The all important Q&A session

- Remember to *not* point with your finger

- Maintain eye contact

- Do not sidetrack question; answer directly. If unsure, admit it or save for a backstage meeting

#2 The all important Q&A session

It's not farfetched to say that most presenters are extremely relieved and extremely worried at the same time when they reach this stage of their speech. They're relieved that most of the talking is now over, but their also deeply anxious about the type of questions that will come flying their way. If you find yourself in this position, remember to keep your cool and remember that the session is *still* within your control.

The general rule of thumb for dealing with questions is to listen to the question, answer it, and then quickly bridge it to your agenda. If you need a minute to think and gather yourself and the answer to your question, repeat the question for the rest of the audience. This also helps the rest of the audience be aware of what exactly you're addressing.

Firstly, when selecting which member of the audience's question to answer, remember to *not* point at them with your finger. In many cultures, this gesture is perceived as rude and aggressive. Instead, gesture at them with your palm faced upward, as if welcoming someone.

While answering the question, remember to maintain eye contact with the person who asked the question. If can, give him/her a concise response and then move on to the next question. Maintain your credibility by offering facts to support your answer and always be diplomatic. If you're asked a question that's unrelated to your topic or completely outside of your field of expertise, you can politely explain the reason to why you're choosing to not answer that question or even covering the topic in your subject. If you find yourself faced with a question asked in an aggressive or particularly argumentative tone, my suggestion is to answer it briefly and quickly, and then immediately move on. Some questioners may try and trap you into a debate which is usually time-consuming and will bore the rest of the audience. Try your very best to avoid falling into an open debate with that individual by rephrasing their question and quickly moving on to the next.

There will also come a time when you find yourself unsure of the answer to someone's question. Truthfully, I believe in being honest and telling him/her that you really aren't sure if the answer you offer may be accurate. However, you can take it an extra mile by promising to gather information about the answer to be sure and get back to them. It's important, then, that obtain that person's contact information from the organizer or the person himself and actually provide him with an answer, or at least an acknowledgment. Alternatively, you can offer the question to other members of the audience and see how they respond. In some situations, you may find yourself greeted with silence the moment you open up the Q&A session. Many speakers immediately move to close the session altogether and exit the stage. I personally think that if you're greeted with silence, you've either (a) lost the audience completely, or (b) got a really shy audience. If you've done everything by the book and how I've advised you to, the latter option is the most definitely the correct answer. If you're speaking to a primarily Asian audience, you're less likely to be bombarded by questions. In that situation, I would suggest *not* closing the session and instead share the answers to some frequently asked questions about your presentation topic. This way you're covering all bases and making sure that you deliver added value to your audience now that the presentation is over.

#3 Getting your audience engaged

- Icebreaker at the start of session

- If group is large, split audience into smaller groups for short activities

- Throw out an open question at the beginning of presentation

#3 Getting your audience engaged

One of the keys to a truly successful presentation is audience participation. By involving your audience in the presentation, you're helping them focus and better-relate to the material you need to present, therefore encouraging them to take immediate action with the ideas you shared after the session. If you're wondering why you need to go the extra mile to get your audience to participate and actually *remember* and apply what you say, let me give you the answer. Your role as a speaker is not just to convey a message, but to also facilitate the absorption and the application of this message. A truly successful speaker truly cares for the audience.

One of the fastest and simplest ways to stimulate audience participation is in the form of an ice-breaker at the very start of the session. Ice-breakers are particularly useful for long seminars, but can also be used in shorter presentations to allow your audience to move around and shake things up before you actually begin. A good ice breaker is to start with asking all members of your audience to stand up and introduce themselves to at least 2 people around them and offer a short, quirky, random fact about themselves.

If you've got time and a large group, you can split your audience into small or partner groups and involve everyone in various activities. In order to fully maximize audience participation, you can even get these groups to elect a leader or a representative to share their findings and voice their unanimous thoughts.

During long sessions, it's easy for the audience to get either groggy or antsy. What you can do is to get them to start your session with warm-up exercises. Ask them to stand up, raise their arms up, and swing about, or even allow them to have a nice cat stretch. Another quirky way of getting them involved, interacting and awake is to get everyone to stand up and give the person next to them a 2-minute back rub. You can also get them up and moving by playing upbeat music and getting them in the groove for a quick shake and dance before you actually begin.

Another good way to actually connect with your audience and get them to interact with *you* is to throw out a question to them at the beginning of your presentation. A common but smart question is to ask them what they expect to gain from your session or speech and at the end of the session, you can review these points with members of your audience to show exactly what you've covered. This is a good way to allow your audience to connect the dots by themselves and actively search your presentation for key takeaways.

In some occasions, you may find yourself wishing to gather input from your audience. Let me share with you a simple and effective method to do so. This method is called the "Ben Franklin Close". The only materials you need are a whiteboard or flip chart and a marker. You start off by splitting the paper into two lengthwise and labeling each side of the paper - pros and cons for example. Then, you get your audience to shout out answers and ideas while you write them down. This not only stimulates their tired brains and gets them thinking, it also gives you a moment to quickly analyze your presentation, recoup, and decide on your next actions.

It's not unusual to be faced with awkward, less-sociable members of the audience. In more conservative cultures, open and casual communication and interaction is not the norm. In order to avoid awkward silences and stony glances, you can pre-select a handful of volunteers. This gives them time to prepare, and fills an other-wise overly quiet session. In the situation where you have no response to your question, be prepared to actually answer it yourself. However, it's important to not take the silence too personally. Every public speaker has faced a stony or less sociable audience at a point in time.

One good way to encourage interaction is through "bribes". No, I'm not talking about the illegal kind. I'm referring to small "secret" gifts you can throw out to more bold and daring members of your audience to "reward" them for their participation. This can include inexpensive custom pens, notepads, folders or even keychains.

Last but not least, you have to remember that the goal of audience involvement and interaction is to inspire them to feel good about themselves and to motivate them to take action. Remember that people act for their own reasons, not yours. Therefore it's important to provide them with an environment within which they can act in response to your message.

Just a quick summary -- introduce ice-breakers into your session, suggest warm-up exercises or dance sessions to keep an upbeat and high flow of energy, get to know your audience and what they want to help them achieve their goals, offer small, inexpensive gifts to get them to participate and remember the goal of audience interaction.

#4 Items of preparation prior to your presentation

- Use cue cards

- Rehearse your opening and ending thoroughly and constantly

- Mind your uhms and ahs (aka 'brain farts')

- Monitor your audience

#4 Items of preparation prior to your presentation

Now that you've covered the basics of speech preparation, speech personalization, vocal energy, body language and platform skills, audience surveying and audience engagement and interaction, you can move on to the final part of this course - the key items you need to get ready prior to your presentation. Here are a few quick tips to help make your presentation smooth-flowing.

First up, use cue cards. If you're unsure of your ability to memorize an entire speech, don't fret - no one really expects you to. With paper, you can easily create quick, point-formed cue cards to help you through an entire presentation. Many public speakers make the mistake of printing an *entire essay* on a bunch of cards. Do not fall into that trap. Remember the outline of your speech that you made at the very beginning of the speech-crafting process? Get that outline and flesh it out into a handful of cue cards. Sprinkle short notes and reminders like "Tell funny pool story" or "Show chart about gender differences" throughout your cue cards instead of the full story itself. Cue cards are extremely useful elements in any presentation and like any other speaker out there, don't hesitate to employ the correct use of it.

Rehearse your opening and ending thoroughly and constantly. I said this before, and I will repeat it again because this is how important it is - Introduction is King. Remember that the first few minutes, or even *seconds*, of your speech determines the mood and flow of the rest of your presentation... and it even determines the amount of audience focus and attention.

Do not over-rehearse. Remember that it's really important to be natural. Rehearsing too much shows, and not in a good way either. While preparation *is* key, you need to make sure that your presentation is conversational and natural, not memorized. Rehearse the full speech the night before your presentation, and then stop. Enough. Forget it.

Mind your uhms and ahs. That may sound silly, but in retrospect, it really isn't. You may not notice your ahs and uhms, but trust me -- your audience does. Watch what you say and keep them to a minimum.

Monitor your audience. The moment you sense that you're losing them and they're phasing out of the presentation, adjust your speech, improvise and project yourself forcefully. Alternatively, at this point of the presentation, you can quickly break and get them to get up and get moving with a quick warm up exercise before quickly repeating your initial points and moving on to the next one.

#4 Items of preparation prior to your presentation

- Get a good night's sleep the night before

- On the day of your presentation, **arrive early**

- Lastly, but most importantly, **have fun!**

Get a good night's sleep the night before. Why do I say that and why is it important? Because lack of sleep results in frayed nerves -- and that shows. When your not sufficiently rested, you're more likely to succumb to nerves, hand jitters and stutters -- all of which damage not only your presentation, but your credibility. Avoid all that and if you're not a coffee-person, don't try to compensate for the lack of sleep with a cup of coffee. You'll find that caffeine does not *just* keep you awake, it keeps you overstimulated and less composed.

On the day of your presentation, arrive early. There are many benefits to arriving early. Firstly, you won't enter the venue like a rushed wreck and waltz onto the stage unprepared. Arriving early allows you to run your points quickly in your mind prior to actually presenting. You'll also come across as cool, calm and collected - important components in conveying confidence. When you're not rushed, you're also less likely to forget things. Secondly, like I said before in this session, arriving early allows you to mingle with your audience and get to know them better. Stand outside while they're registering and converse with them. Find out their hopes and dreams and know what they hope to gain from your session, or even why they attended at all. Simple things like that not only help you determine the tone of your presentation, but allow your audience to connect with you and get to know you. This way, you *know* that you already have friends in the audience and will be less likely to fear and be nervous.

Lastly, but most importantly, have fun. It may sound impossible, but there are neurons in your brain called "mirror neurons". Like their names, they mirror the actions of the person before you. If your energy is high and your tone upbeat, your audience will mirror the exact same thing. Vice versa if your energy is low and your tone monotonous - they will mirror boredom. You need to enjoy what you're talking about, and inject passion and enthusiasm into your presentation. In other words... you need to have fun.

Unit 2: Better Public Speaking

Introduction to Public Speaking

Can you think of any memorable talk or presentation you have ever attended? It is sad to know that most of the presentations are easy to forget, especially when the main reason behind the presentation was to communicate something to you.

But if you remember these four basic things, then be assured that your verbal messages will be understood and remembered for long. Though these things may sound somewhat obvious and deceptively simple, they are of immense importance.

1. You should understand your presentation's purpose.
2. Don't confuse things; keep your message clear and exact.
3. Be prepared well to face the audience and their questions.
4. Don't be monotonous; instead be vivid while giving the speech.

Always be clear about the idea that what do you want to achieve. It is very essential for you to know and understand, before you start working on your presentation or speech, what you want to say, whom you want to approach as your audience and why is it important for them to listen. Ask basic questions to yourself such as whom do you want to speak to, what are their interests, their beliefs and principles, what is common between them and others and how do they differ.

What is the message you want to convey to your audience? You can answer this question by asking yourself about the 'success criteria'. How will you come to know whether and when your message has been successfully communicated?

Which is the best way to put across your message? Here non verbal cues such as your expressions and body language play a vital role along with the language. But keep your audience in mind while deciding your words and non-verbal cues. Plan your presentation from its start to the end. If you can add, then prepare audio-visuals to grab the audience's attention.

The timing is also very important. Your contributions are seen and heard as relevant to the issue only if you develop a sense of timing. You should know when the time to speak is and when is it the time to be silent.

Next important question is 'where?' You should bear in mind the physical context of the communication. In case you are using audio or visual aids, then check for availability and the visibility. Visit the venue if you can.

To ensure that your audience listens to you and not just hear, you must know why they should be listening and tell them so if it is necessary.

Maintain simplicity. When you are conveying your message, use less but powerful words to leave a better impact. When you start giving too much of the information to the audience, they get overloaded and thus, tend to get bored.

In case you are using slides, use simple single statement or a diagram to convey your message, limit your content.

Be thoroughly prepared. If you fail to prepare, then you are prepared to fail. It is indeed an important aspect that decides your success as a speaker. In order to give yourself time to prepare your speech, set timing for meeting, speaking and presentation well in advance.

Since all communications cannot be scheduled, preparation may lead to good and thorough understanding.

How to achieve successful delivery of speech? How you represent yourself, your speech and the presentation leave a long lasting impression up on the audience. Only way to achieve success here is by practicing hard. Here are some tips to hold your audience's attention:

1. Associate your speech to the life by stating instances and citing examples.
2. Don't just stand and give your speech, bring in some animation, use your body language.
3. Give pauses where ever you can. Don't talk too fast or else the audience won't be able to understand you.
4. Use voice modulation. Stress on main points and use various tones of voice.
5. If possible, use audio and visual aids.

Though public speaking and presentations appear to be a daunting task, but they can be turned into an enjoyable and a rewarding experience once you have practiced and rehearsed well. Always be a confident and an enthusiastic speaker.

Getting Started

If you 'have' to or if you 'want' to make a eulogy speech so as to express your inner feelings you have, in public, for your near and dear one who has just left the world, then read this article.

It is very much understandable that such a time is really very tough to compose a eulogy speech or maybe anything else. It is a hard time and you find it difficult to focus as you are distressed. But it is fine. Here are a few simple and easy tips which can help you write a nice eulogy speech:

Adding a story or a communication that you have shared with the deceased is one of the best element to put in the eulogy speech. It can be any, a funny or a heart-wrenching one. You can do with one of each type also. But it is great to have a single story that has both the elements. It is not mandatory for you to tell only one story.

You can start your eulogy with an incident re-counting how you interacted with your loved one. You can even talk about an incidence that you will remember for a lifetime of them that you had when you were a child. Or you can tell about an important lesson of life that you have learnt from them and how helpful it has been in your journey.

One of the benefits of adding a story in your eulogy speech is that since you have lived that moment there is no need for you to memorize and read the words. You have a vivid memory of it. Since you have been through that moment, all you need to do is to make a rough outline of the incident or make brief bullet points in your notes. Then during the speech you can begin about it by saying anything that briefly reminds you of the anecdote you wish to share.

There are some other things too that you need to remember while composing a eulogy speech. But to assist you while you get started and to eradicate the pressure of creating a lovely and a great tribute to your loved one, the story will be an excellent idea.

Tom Antion is a renowned speech expert and is also the author of a book called "Instant Eulogy Speeches". This book helps you write a nice eulogy speech even though you are downright upset and depressed. It also contains very lovely photographs and phrases that you can use in your finished eulogy. You can also add many more pieces of appropriate humor so as to ease the tension of the atmosphere.

Get Rid of Your Speaking Fear

You can reduce your fear of speaking in the public by simply adopting some of the following tips.

1. Conduct a thorough research on your topic. To meet the expectation of the audience, visit or call the key participants and have a chat with them. Get to know what they expect from your presentation, what they want to learn and what do they already know. Then prepare your presentation accordingly so that it benefits them. These sorts of conversations help you learn and know what your audience expects from you and thus give you the advantage of preparing accordingly beforehand.

2. Prepare well. Don't write down the whole speech, but a rough outline with the help of the keywords. Then rehearse as much as you can. Be assured that you are able to deliver your speech in a conversational manner without reading the script. Do not memorize it word for word. It will make it sound robotic and dull. Moreover it makes things complicated. Just in case you forget a point you may keep on stumbling in your speech. So avoid it. Keep practicing your speech anywhere and anytime you find it possible.

3. Rehearse well for it. Keep on practicing your speech among a group of friends or coworkers and if possible even with your boss. Ask them about their views on your speech and try to improve accordingly. Also take advantage of this opportunity to get familiar with the room and equipments. This helps you face the audience confidently.

4. Always play a gentle and an amicable host. Get friendly with your audience by arriving early at the venue and greeting them beforehand. Some simple gestures such as shaking hands with them and thanking them for coming can help you build up a warm rapport with them. Try to engage them in a simple talk with you by introducing yourself and asking them about their well being, etc. Convert the strangers into friends and make them feel comfortable.

5. Always expect success. If you expect it, then you will definitely work hard to achieve it too. Fantasize yourself doing a wonderful job with perfection. Never scare yourself with nightmares. When you expect yourself to do well, you gain confidence. Remember that everyone expects you to do an excellent job.

Making a Fluent Speech

Do you stammer when you have to speak in front of someone or a gathering?

Then this article is meant for you. If you are looking forward to achieve fluency, read on. This article will interest you as it looks at the speech impediment such as stammering and stuttering. I am Steve Hill. Since the age of four I have been suffering with a stutter. Though I had regular conventional speech therapy sessions, I continued to stutter till the age of twenty two.

Life was extremely frustrating when I used to stutter. But there were times when I could speak very well too. Whenever I used to speak to my ex- girlfriend, I rarely ever stuttered. But it was quite disheartening that when I attempted to speak to her parents, I struggled quite a lot.

I noticed that whenever I was drunk, my fluency level used to improve tremendously and at that time if I used to stutter, it came to me as a shock!

I could never deduce that why I used to stutter talking to some person when I was totally fluent speaking to the other. Also I found it hard to understand that why I could speak without any problem when I was drunk and stutter when I was sober.

Tired of my situation, I read as many books as I could find about speech impediments and achieving fluency and stuttering. I also made contacts with some of the speech therapists. After having read these books and conversing with the therapists, I was told and was made to believe that I could not lead a stuttering free life as it suggested that you are unable to eradicate stutter.

It was indeed a negative attitude and I could not accept what I was hearing and reading because I knew that I was able to talk very well without stuttering at all at times.

One day while watching television I came across Bruce Willis' interview. Now I consider myself fortune enough to have seen it. In that interview Bruce Willis stated that he too suffered from the problem of stuttering which started when he was a young boy. However by the time he reached his late teenage, he had managed to attain fluency. I was inspired by it tremendously and it was then that I decided that I would attempt and overcome my speech impediment.

It took a year's intense labor and hard work for me to overcome my speech impediment. I never lost the hope and kept thinking positive. Pouring over books and by basically studying the people whom I thought were great speakers, I managed to beat my stutter. Now I have made it my career, I help people achieve fluency.

Keeping Your Audience Attentive

To highlight the occasion, be it award ceremonies, conventions, alumni, fund raising, homecomings, commencement exercise etc., guest speakers are usually invited. Guest speakers are usually selected according to their accomplishments and popularity so as to make the gathering a memorable one.

In order to be successful and impart a lasting image in the eyes of the audience, a speaker must find out techniques and methods to keep the audience's attention glued to his speech. The following are a few methods you can stick to:

1. Always speak in enthusiastic tone and remember to keep your voice clear, crisp and comprehensible. Try not to stumble in your speech or eat words in between.

2. The speech you make at such gatherings must be in consonance with its aim and should touch the issues related and relevant to its purpose and valid to present needs for the advantage of the greater part.

3. Many speakers prefer a list of subjects they want to discuss instead of preparing, memorizing and

rehearsing the whole speech word for word. An impulsive speech aligned on the subjects listed is projected more naturally.

4. To keep the audience attentive and at tender hooks, inject humor into your speech. But bear in mind to keep humor up to a decent level so that unintentionally you may not embarrass others or get yourself misunderstood by them.

5. The best way to raise an issue is by citing examples and instances. Clearly associate the example and the issue so as to make the audience understand better.

6. If you are to make a speech in a gathering that has been organized to save an industry or boost the morale of those associated with it either directly or indirectly, try and deliver a stimulating and motivating speech. To turn the mood from depressing to enthusiastic one, include some inspirational words and positive thoughts that will project a bright and happy tomorrow.

7. Your speech may sound more of a discussion if you involve the audience but in one way it will confirm the usefulness of what you are saying and offering.

8. Always be precise and realistic in your projection of the industry in positive flight five or ten years from now on. Call for hard work is need be.

9. The best way to wrap up your speech is by leaving a lasting and meaningful message for the audience to ponder up on.

To make the audience remember you even long after the speech has been made, say significant stuff giving food to the audience's brain.

Have you ever been put to sleep by a boring speaker? While you fight the urge to slip happily into your dreamland, your head is nodding though paying the least attention.

Though many of you will not admit it but sure this has happened to all of us at least once. But don't ever let it happen when you are the speaker. The only way to keep your audience alive and active while you are making a speech is to interact with them and involve them into it. There are various ways to involve your audience:

1. Ask questions to the audience. It will make them work their brains and think of an answer. If you feel that people are losing interest, simply put up a question and select someone from the audience to answer it. Whether you get the answer or not thank that person and proceed to someone else in the audience. This keeps the audience active both mentally and physically.

2. Always finish the sentence. If you just begin a famous sentence such as "Lions and tigers and bears…" and leave it midway, only those people familiar to the movie "The Wizard of Oz" will be able to respond to you. Always choose something that is obvious for them to guess.

3. Whenever you feel that the room is heavy with energy, change it using this simple technique. Ask a simple question and then question "Is this good stuff?" And as the audience replies with a "Yes", you tell them to turn to people on their either side

and give them a high-five and say this aloud 'this is good stuff'. It really makes them get a kick out of it.

4.   According to a famous millionaire, T. Harv Ecker you should get your audience to do the work for you. In order to achieve this, break your audience into groups of two or three and then hand over some exercises to them that are an integral part of your presentation. In order to tempt your audience to remain active and participate reward them for the same. Ask questions to the audience and then whoever answers; just reward them with a candy. People compete for it and hence, it becomes a game. Use it only for a few minutes in the middle of your talk.

There are plenty of other ways to involve your audience. You as a speaker should come up with various new techniques that you feel are appropriate for your audience and for you.

Presenting Without PowerPoint

It is easy to make presentations today, thanks to PowerPoint. In order to make the process of teaching and learning easy and fun filled, teachers and lecturers use presentations. Still there are professionals who follow their age-old beliefs for presentations and thus make them without using PowerPoint.

It is boring to have presentations without the use of PowerPoint. Minus the musical background and visual aids, the presentation appears quite monotonous. With the help of PowerPoint there comes in a huge change for the audience in the presentation. Thus, the use of creativity is essential in the presentations being made without the aid of PowerPoint.

To give a successful presentation without the use of PowerPoint, always remember to be precise and exact about what you are talking. Remember to first understand and learn the disposition and nature of the audience and then make your presentation.

Always present the beginning of the presentation by keeping in mind the end of it. Without PowerPoint you might lose the interest of the audience soon, so always remember the purpose of your presentation. To leave a lasting image, make a strong start. Since you are presenting without PowerPoint, always remember to set the right tone among the audience to listen to you throughout your presentation by carefully planning your first words and appearance.

One of the most important things to remember is to work on your speech as much as possible because without the visual treat that the PowerPoint offers, whatever you say and the way you make your speech is detrimental. Only practice can make a person a successful speaker.

Props can also be used to make a presentation, without PowerPoint. Look interesting because a prop may convey a message more easily and substantially. As long as it conveys the message, it works as an effective tool.

By bringing in the solutions to the problem you are discussing in your presentation, you can grab the attention of the audience, even though you are not using the PowerPoint. As you have already researched the audience, you would already know their problem and all you will need to do is to bring in new ideas to make them try it.

The only visual aid for the audience, if you are not using the PowerPoint, is you. So minus the PowerPoint, the success of the presentation depends solely on the speaker as there are no fancy slides to drive them off the speaker. So the speaker needs to be self confident and well versed in his speech.

Handling Public Speaking Question

The deciding factor as to how your presentation is received by the audience is how you handle the questions put up by the audience. It becomes all the more important if you are pitching for business.

1. Always be prepared for the questions. When you are preparing for your speech or presentation, think about the questions that are likely to be put up and then prepare your answers.

2. Make it clear in your mind as to when do you want to take up the questions, along with your presentation or at the end of it. Choose whatever suits you but then don't change, once you have decided.

3. Never end your presentation with questions. Always ask for questions at least five to ten minutes before the end, deal with them and end by summarizing because if you don't get any questions then the end of your presentation becomes a bit flat.

4. Whenever a question is popped at you, listen to it carefully and do look like you are listening. You might have faced the same questions innumerable times before but remember to treat your questioner with respect and don't play down their question.

5. Always thank your questioner. It's polite and shows respect. It also lends you time to ponder upon your answer.

6.   Repeat the questions aloud as many of the people in the audience might not have heard and thus it may not make any sense to them. It also makes you look in control and clever.

7.   Answer to everyone in the audience and not just to the questioner. Most of the time what happens is, if the questioner is in the front, the speaker ends up having conversation with him/her and excludes everyone else.

8.   Always try and keep it simple. By the time you reach the question part of your presentation, most of the audience have become relaxed and thus might drag the session with too many questions.

9.   Don't try to bluff your audience. If someone asks you a question to which you don't know the answer, simply tell them and assure them that you will get back to them after you have found out the answer.

It might be possible that no one from the audience asks any question which leaves an awkward silence. People might need some time to get what you have said and then ask. But to avoid that awkward silence you may ask some questions to yourself and then head for the summary and closing statement.

Avoiding Panic Attacks

Many people dread speaking in public and hence associate with panic attack. It is possible that they might have had an anxiety-producing public speaking experience. It has been noticed that people who frequently have to speak in public, suffer from panic attacks.

Here is a very interesting story about a girl named Amber. Amber, when entered into high school had many risk factors for panic attacks. Until her final semester, Amber was somehow successful at avoiding a speech class. But to graduate, she was supposed to take a speech. Amber was always dreading the idea of taking up public speaking class, though she had never received any diagnosis of panic attacks or anxiety disorder. Even the idea of standing up facing a class full of her peers was enough to make her feel dizzy and nauseous.

Even the teacher could see how very nervous Amber was, as she walked into her first day of the public speaking class. He approached her after the class and conversed with her about her obvious discomfort. Amber elaborated her physical reaction to her teacher, in regard to public speaking. She explained to the teacher how she gets extremely anxious and feel nauseous and dizzy even at the idea of speaking in front of her peers and becomes short breathed.

The teacher recommended her to visit the school counselor before coming to their next class. This made Amber feel embarrassed and she became even more anxious at the thought of meeting the counselor.

However the school counselor was very much familiar with the symptoms of panic attack and knew well that the students feel uncomfortable to discuss about it in front of their friends. In order to make Amber face her next day of speech class, the counselor advised her to stand up in front of her family whenever she wanted to talk.

Amber told her family what she was trying to do to overcome her fear of speaking in the public. That night at dinner, every time Amber wanted to have an item passed to her, she stood up. Speaking in front of her family was a lot different than speaking in front of her peers, but that practice enabled her to get through her next class without any full blown panic attack.

One night before she had a big speech due, Amber asked a few of her friends to come to her home. She wanted to practice her speech in front of them and her family until she was sure to get through it sans any amount of anxiety. This technique is called systematic desensitization. It is indeed one of the most widely used techniques to get people rid of panic attacks.

Overcome the Confidence Killers

To become a confident person, all one has to do is to eradicate the confidence killers. The self-defeating thought patterns are called as confident killers. Many of us believe in these harmful suppositions. Here are a few confidence killers mentioned, see if you have any:

1. Do you consider yourself as the "All for Nothing" sniper? If you believe so, then probably it is the biggest reason why you never seem to enjoy even your smallest victories that you have achieved in life. You think of yourself as someone who is a complete failure if you have failed to achieve perfection. If you stop being so hard to yourself, you might become a confident person.

2. Never think that there is always a disaster waiting for you. Don't let the Dark Cloud of Destruction make you think silly things. Believe in yourself and move ahead.

3. The next confident killer is 'Warlord of Negative Magnification'. If you pay heed to this one, you won't ever be able to overcome your lack of confidence. It's simple and makes you believe that if this is something good, it doesn't really count. You

will build up more and more negative energy starting from a tiny speck by magnifying it like a mountain. For instance, suppose you have won eight contests but you failed to achieve success in the ninth one, then don't think about the one you lost, but instead look at the eight achievements. Doing the other way round makes you kill your confidence.

4.	Never go by the thought that if you feel it then it must be so. It blocks the clear thinking parts of your brain. It is not always that what you feel is actually the truth. No one can be perfect always; we all have some days when we are not able to perform to the perfection. Don't let your emotions over run your lives. Be confident that maybe next day you will be better.

5.	Perfectionists are bound to be good at making 'should statements'. But what one must remember is that should statements are more about what, according to you, is expected by the people from you and not what you really want. Taking an example, if someone makes a statement that everyone should have an education plan. Then the people who don't have an education plan might fret at this thought and think that there is something wrong with them.

6.	Don't label yourself as a loser. Never say that you are a loser or everything went wrong because of you. If you have to label yourself, then better label yourself as a confident person. Throw away this libelous labeler attitude.

<ol start="7">
<li>Never be a compliment constrictor, this won't ever allow you to accept a compliment. It will instead make you feel you are not worth it.</li>
</ol>

If you are able to find out your confidence killer(s) from these, then half of the battle is over. The only thing that is now left is to train yourself in order to abandon these confidence-killing thoughts.

Secrets to build confidence

We need to build up our confidence from time to time. How we feel about ourselves has a lot to do with feeling confident. To feel confident, we should have this feeling that we can achieve the goals we have set for ourselves.

Everyone has been gifted with one or the other talent. To think like a winner we must feel confident that we are good in these skills. Below are a few ways given to train yourself to think like a winner:

Prepare a "to-do" list for yourself. Never complain that you have tried something before and that it did not work. It is this list that can make you feel like a winner. Always make a list that is fun and easy to get done so that it makes you feel like a winner. The list can be utterly easy too so that even after doing these small jobs; a confidence is developed in you.

It is more of a self-conditioning list. When at the end of the day you see all the check marks on your "to-do" list, it makes you feel that you have had a productive day. You gain confidence as you find out your abilities of having things get done.

You come to think yourself as a winner after having done the things you have listed on your fun list. In case you have forgotten to make a list at the beginning of the day, make a list of the things you have done in that day and at the end of it, mark them off.

This fun "to-do" list of yours may sound as a silly technique to build up self confidence, but remember that the subconscious part of our mind doesn't bother what is real and what is imaginary. All that matters to that part of your mind is that you are accomplishing something every day by making sure you have done everything that you have listed. Slowly and gradually you will notice a change in your confidence level. As it starts to mount, add up some real tasks in your list and do them with the same 'feel-good' attitude.

As you are just beginning, don't add too many tasks. Disguise your real tasks that you want to achieve with the easy ones. Feeling good is an important element in building up of confidence so even these small accomplishments help boost your confidence immensely. If you know someone who is a very confident person, then look up to them. They are always smiling. So have fun in your life and enjoy it. It will definitely make you feel like a winner.

Successful Public Speech

Many people avoid and dread speaking in public. But like all other fears, we need to overcome this one too. It has been a common observation that many people tend to get nervous before and during their speech or presentation.

It is often recommended to practice meditation or take regular breaths whenever you feel nervous. Since it's a natural reaction, it is good to take few deep breaths to help you relax before starting your speech or presentation.

Before starting your speech, make sure you have a focal point in the room which will act to give you inspiration and will keep you motivated. There are times when you get distracted midway and you lose your focus, at this time the focal point may help you get back.

When you are giving a public speech, try not to look at the eyes of the people in the audience as it might put you off. Although you have to plan what you are about to say in the speech but never plan it word for word. Make it look natural by making your speech spontaneous touching the points you have listed and want to discuss.

You can even start your speech with a public joke in order to break the ice. Sometime back I gave a speech in the company where I worked. People in my office brought some presents and put to a collection and I had to say a few words to thanks them. I was aware of the fact that I have to give a speech, many weeks in advance, and that put me in quite a bit of stress.

The speech was to be made in front of around fifty people and was supposed to last for ten minutes. I began my speech by saying thanks to those who had put to the collection, and to add humor I added, "and to those who haven't I will see you outside." Though it was quite a pathetic joke, a few people laughed and it was this that made me relax and gave me extra confidence.

I would also advise that when you are delivering a public speech always talk a bit slower than normal. I hope as it had helped me immensely over the years it will work the same way for you.

I hope after having read this article you will be able to deliver a quality public speech.

Get a standing ovation by presenting a lively speech

To bring a page of written context to spoken life, presentation techniques are essential. To inject interest in the audience and build up a rapport use your body language to animate your presentation. Here are few techniques which you can follow to keep the audience's glued to your speech:

1. As you are speaking to the audience, the way you speak is of significant importance and so are the words that you choose.

    a) Avoid using technical, bureaucratic and tough language. Instead of long phrases, use short and meaningful sentences.

    b) Be very specific. Prefer giving a specific day or time rather than saying "soon".

    c) Try to use concrete words over abstract ones. For example, use the word "microphone" over "sound amplification facilities"

    d) Use simple language rather than Latinized words.

2. Instead of technical, use conversational English. Speaking the words from the prepared text sounds very robotic, artificial and stilted. On the other hand, use of conversational English makes the speech sound natural and flowing. It also helps to build up a rapport with the audience.

Conversational English differs from the written one very distinctly. In conversational English, grammatical and incorrect use of words can be ignored as long as the message has been clearly delivered. Use colloquial language.

3. Everything you say should make sense. There is a major difference in expressing the same sentence by writing and by speaking. A listener is solely dependent on the speaker to make him understand.

4. To make it more interesting, use the technique of labeling and signposting in your presentation. It enables to know what is coming up next and make them know what you really want them to understand from it.

   a) You can signpost the whole talk at the beginning itself by telling the audience what all are you going to discuss.
   b) You can even signpost the sub-points of the issue to be discussed.
   c) You can signpost the issue itself.
   d) Or you can signpost the end of your presentation.

5. You can use jokes as an amusing way to build a rapport with the audience. The shared laughter becomes a point of contact. But jokes need to be well-presented, appropriate and funny, as; if it works it brings you together but if it fails it pushes you apart. Have good comic timing and don't forget the punch-line.

6. Pause to give an extra effect to your speech. But you need to know when it is appropriate to give a pause and let your message to sink in.

   a) You can pause to tease your audience after a provocative question.
   b) You can pause before you deliver the punch-line of your joke.

c) You can add a pause to let your audience re-settle after a general discussion or laughter.

d) You can pause to give your audience time to think about any question you might have asked.

e) You can also use a slightly longer pause to show that you are in control.

7. Don't just keep on telling the audience; add a touch to your presentation by converting a point into a narrative or a story so as to entertain your audience and involve them into it.

Mastering such simple techniques can raise your presentation expertise to great heights!

Unit 3: Public Speaking: Terror to Triumph

INTRODUCTION

Spoken language is a fundamental element of human relationships. The ability to use words effectively can help you achieve great things in life. Oral presentations are the cornerstone of human interaction on a large scale and they also have a profound effect on intimate interactions as well.

Speaking in public can be a great source of anxiety for many people. However, it doesn't have to be. People have been practicing this art for centuries and it has become an integral part of our interactions today.

Some approach public speaking like a type of internal thrill ride while others are choked silent at the very thought of giving a speech. Overcoming the fear of speaking in public is a subject of great interest to many. This activity is rated among the most frightening events in a person's life. Some have gone as far as rating the fear of public speaking higher than the fear of death.

Many people are able to overcome their fear of speaking in front of an audience in spite of its seemingly overwhelming nature. The process begins with a strong understanding of how public speaking functions.

This text focuses on defining public speaking in a way that can help you get a handle on your fears. It is also designed to help you create strategies that will give you the means to create an effective oral presentation whether you are directing a video conference or giving a toast during a special occasion.

PUBLIC SPEAKING

Public speaking is simply the act of talking in front of a group of people. The group can be quite small or impressively large. In either case, many individuals find the process to be overwhelming.

Speaking in public is an art. Effective presentations require clear delivery that includes proper inflection, pauses and emphasis. Some people seem to have the knack for oral presentation while others struggle with this type of activity.

Natural talent does help. However, effective public speaking can be achieved with research and diligent practice. The art of oral presentation is one that can be mastered with the right methods and persistence.

This form of communication is also a science. An oral presentation is most effective when it is well structured and purposeful. Those who take a scientific approach that involves a methodical system can do as well as ones who are accidentally talented.

Oral presentations serve a number of purposes. They can entertain. They can be used to influence others and they can simply be informative. The purpose of the talk will have great bearing on how the speaker will organize his thoughts, information and emotive components.

FIVE ELEMENTS OF SPEAKING IN PUBLIC

It is said that people wear different masks for different occasions. We change our mannerisms in various environments. When speaking in public, there are some considerations that need to be made in order to plan the presentation well.

The first element of public speaking is the person delivering the lecture. The speaker should carefully consider how he wants to be perceived by the audience. The beauty of this type of venture is that you can create a persona that suits your presentation.

The second element is the message. It is important to consider the information you are presenting. The content is of immense value for any oral presentation. Well organized subject matter is an integral part of a successful public speaking event.

The method is the third element to consider. Where will the speech be delivered? What prompt will be used? Will there be visual and sound aids? Is the presentation in a formal setting, a conference room or a casual setting?

The final element concerns the purpose of the presentation. Is it designed to inform? Is there an entertainment value to the piece? Is the presentation supposed to motivate and influence the audience?

BRIEF HISTORY OF PUBLIC SPEAKING

The art and science of speaking in public is deeply rooted in civilizations across the globe. The spoken word is of great value and it has been for centuries. This fundamental mode of communication has helped mankind progress through the ages.

Before writing was incorporated as a method of communicating, oral presentations were of the utmost importance. Many valuable written works were committed to memory and recited over and over again for audiences to enjoy.

Poetry evolved as a necessary method of effective memorization. Those who created oral presentations and stories would rhyme the words in order to make them easier to memorize. This useful literary device has persevered over time into an art form of its own.

The spoken word was of great influence on various civilizations over time. Public discourse, debate and discussions had a profound effect in nearly every aspect of life. Religion, politics and entertainment are just a few examples of venues that relied on oral presentations.

PUBLIC SPEAKING TODAY

Today, public speaking remains a driving force in many different realms of our daily lives. Oral presentations continue to inform, influence and entertain us. We rely on spoken words in our most fundamental dealings with family members and as a mode of connecting with one another on a global level.

The advancements of technology have given rise to effective communication on a grand scale. Word-of-mouth previously took days, months or even years to travel effectively. Technology provides ways of spreading spoken language across the globe in an instant.

With some of today's public speaking venues, like videoconferencing, the speaker can deliver a presentation to hundreds or even thousands of people without facing the audience at all. Telecommunications has paved the way for effective communication to the masses with little or no contact.

Something does get lost in the process. The audience can be a very valuable tool in an oral presentation. The loss of this advantageous resource can leave some speakers at a loss. Others may find the prospect of speaking to a camera preferable to speaking to a live audience.

OCCASIONS AND EVENTS

The delivery of your message can be completed via telecommunications. You may find yourself staring into a blank lens that offers no feedback. Other occasions may call for you to create a stellar oral presentation to a handful of co-workers.

Some events may call on your ability to inform the audience. You concise informative speech may be designed to covey an important message about safety issues in the workplace. You may be in charge of influencing a number of people to vote on a certain issue.

Other events are more personal. Maybe you need to deliver an unforgettable speech at your best friend's wedding. You may simply want to hone your skills in order to effectively convey your thoughts to friends, loved ones and associates on a day-to-day basis.

FEARS AND PHOBIAS

Though the very thought of speaking in front of a crowd is overwhelming, it is important to take time to make a clear distinction between fears and phobias. You may find that you are more than simply afraid of the task. If you have a phobia then there are other precautions that you need to take.

Fear can be such a prominent emotion that you may feel confused about possibly having a phobia. After delving into the similarities and differences you may come up with a valid conclusion on your own. You may also want to consult a professional if you feel that you truly do have a phobia.

FEAR

Fear is a fundamental emotion that serves a very important purpose. This particular emotion is designed for self preservation. Without fear, people may engage in activities that are far too dangerous. Survival of the human race would be at risk without this necessary emotive force.

In spite of its fundamental nature fear is a very complex emotion that has several sources. This emotion is typically hardwired into our beings to ensure our safety. The severity of the apprehension and anxiety associated with the feeling varies from person to person.

The body has a prominent response to this emotion. Physical changes occur in our bodies when we feel fear. The autonomic nervous system kicks into gear accompanied by the adrenal glands. People can often recognize the feeling of fear by their automatic physical responses.

Trembling, tenseness and rapid breathing are common signs. Increased heart rate, sweating and dry mouth can also accompany this emotion. Blood flows away from the brain to other parts of the body since the energy can be better used to run or stand up to the challenge.

Since the blood can flow away from the brain rather quickly some may experience lightheadedness and fainting during extreme fear experiences. The fight or flight response is also commonly activated during substantially fearful situations. This response tells the body to either flee or protect one's self through force.

Fear can also be learned. There is some debate as to the extent that this emotion is naturally hardwired for self preservation and to what extent it is learned. The environment can play a crucial role in a person's prominent fears but it is not clear how much of the emotion is learned and how much is naturally integrated into the human body.

PHOBIA

A phobia is a very specific fear that is excessive. The irrational nature of the fear along with the unwarranted response distinguishes this condition from typical fearful reactions.

Phobias are relatively common. However, they can be classified as psychological disorders in some cases.

In order for a condition to be classified as a disorder it has to interfere with the individual's ability to function normally on a day-to-day basis. For example, a phobia of high places may not in itself qualify as a disorder. A phobia of high places that prevents a person from walking up and down steps would be a disorder.

THREE TYPES OF PHOBIAS

There are three basic types of phobias recognized by the Diagnostic and Statistical Manual of Mental Disorders. Simple phobias are irrational fears of objects or situations. Social phobias consists of fear of social situations and agoraphobia is the fear of being trapped in a situation or setting.

- *Simple phobias*

Simple phobias come in a variety of forms and they can include just about any object or situation. The individual tends to have an overwhelming feeling that he needs to avoid these object or situations. He also recognizes that the fear is irrational. Those who fall into this category do not always seek treatment for their conditions.

- *Agoraphobia*

Agoraphobia was formally classified as a fear of open spaces. However, more recent developments recognize that individuals who have this condition avoid leaving their homes because they are afraid of being trapped. It is believed that agoraphobia develops as a result to panic attacks. The person is afraid of having an attack in a pubic place or an inescapable location.

- *Social phobias*

Social phobias are completely overpowering to the individual that has them. Of course, a person with social phobia would be paralyzed at the very thought of speaking in public. The fear of being judged or publicly humiliated is too disabling for the individual.

Phobic conditions are considered to be anxiety disorders. These conditions can be treated with behavior therapy, medications or a combination of the two. Other treatment techniques include gradual exposure to the situation or object (desensitizing) and visualizations.

GLOSSOPHOBIA

There are fundamental differences between fears and phobias. Our fears are necessary components to self preservation. They may seem a little unreasonable at times but they do not interfere with our ability to function normally on a day to day basis.

Phobias are persistent, unreasonable and excessive. The mere thought of being in a certain situation or getting close to a certain object is the source of overwhelming anxiety. The major difference between fear and phobia is impairment.

For example, a person can be afraid to deliver an oral presentation and still function normally. He may perspire, shake and lose his train of thought but he is able to attend the event. He may choose to back out of the speech out of fear but he is still quite capable.

The person who suffers from glossophobia has a very different experience. The very thought of speaking in public results in all-consuming anxiety. Physical distress is exhaustively uncomfortable and includes nausea and feelings of panic. Individuals who have glossophobia avoid any situation that may call for verbal interaction with any group.

The physical responses to glossophobia are closely related to fear's fundamental flight or fight response. The individual experiences accelerated heart rate, increased blood pressure, dry mouth and stiffened muscles. The senses are heightened but they individual may still feel lightheaded and even faint.

Some people can develop speech disorders while trying to speak in public. These include stammering and stuttering. Some may find it difficult to articulate words that usually pose no challenge for them in these situations.

Glossophobia is a condition that is related specifically to public speaking. Some people are able to perform in public through dancing or singing and still have this social phobia. Speech anxiety can be overcome in some situations if the person sees himself as an actor rather than himself as he gives the presentation.

ROOT CAUSES OF PUBLIC SPEAKING FEARS

In order to overcome a fear, it is necessary to recognize the root causes of it. Fear is an important emotion that is designed to help us protect ourselves. Some emotions are hardwired into our system in order to keep us out of danger. Even the fear of public speaking may have roots in self preservation.

Fears can also be learned. We can adopt a fear of a certain situation through our experiences. Some of us find ourselves fearful of an object or circumstance when we see others fearful of it.

Of course, it is obvious that a person is not facing immediate threat of harm when he speaks in public. However, there are components to the emotion that are self-preserving in nature. Fear of public speaking is complex because it seems to be a combination of both instinct and learned fear. To what extent either has influence is unknown.

HARDWIRED FEARS

The fear of public speaking can be considered a natural response to an overwhelming social situation. The negative emotion may have a significant purpose. It can be considered as a mode of self preservation.

Some fears are hardwired into the human system. They help us make sound decisions that can protect us from harm. Fearful reactions are perfectly natural in spite of their negative impact on the body and psyche.

The fundamental message is that there is danger in the immediate surroundings. We are naturally afraid of many indicators of danger. Some include loud noises and high places. Our bodies react in a way that makes us aware that some action is required.

The fear of public speaking can be partially hardwired into the human psyche. Considering the conditions of a public speaking event, there is little wonder why the body has such a profound reaction to the situation. One person faces a crowd of others. This can be a precarious position on a primitive level.

It stands to reason that the body would naturally transfer into a flight or fight response when faced with such a situation. Though you may know that the audience is harmless, you still feel a natural sense that you need to protect yourself. This is part of what makes the fear of public speaking universal to some degree.

LEARNED FEARS

Some fears are learned. Our early experiences teach us to be afraid of various objects and situations. A child may not be afraid of a flame until experience teaches him to be wary. The experiences can come in a number of different forms.

Let's consider the child and the flame. The child may learn to fear this element by experiencing a burn. He can also learn to be afraid of fire if his caretaker exhibits a severe reaction to the element. He can also learn to have a fearful reaction if he sees someone else get burned.

It is important to remember that the mind is a very powerful force that has a profound effect on our fears. A person can imagine an experience that leads to feelings of trepidation in certain situations. A vivid imagination is as influential as an actual experience in many cases.

PUBLIC SPEAKING FEARS

It is natural to feel trepidation when faced with the task of speaking in public. There are also learned elements that come into play. Part of the fear arises from pure imagination. There are also hidden sources as well. Each individual has his own reasons for feeling anxious about speaking in public.

Some may have had a traumatic experience related to public speaking. A negative incident can have life-long implications. A person can learn to be afraid to speak in front of a crowd through experiencing extreme fear in a single experience related to this activity.

Even if the intense fear is felt for just a moment, the impact can last a lifetime. The nervous system is designed to connect fear with situations that should be avoided. Feeling great anxiety and dread during a certain event teaches the body to respond appropriately.

People make strong associations between feelings and events. Some are quick to learn fear in some situations directly. In other instances, the negative feelings may not have anything to do with the act of speaking itself. The individual simply makes the association through the mind.

EMPATHY AND ASSOCIATION

Many people develop a fear of public speaking though association. The person does not experience the negative event personally but he witnesses someone else's negative experience. If the event is traumatic for the observed individual, the subject learns to fear the situation himself.

This empathetic take is similar to a child becoming afraid of dogs after witnessing another child being bitten. The observance of the traumatic incident is enough to create fear in the child.

GRADUAL BUILDING

People can also learn to fear speaking in front of a crowd over time. A very mild case of stage fright can develop into a more serious condition if the individual lets the feeling accumulate over time. If the subject focuses on the fear, the fear will become stronger.

Relatively innocuous experiences can build into feelings of overwhelming fear. The body learns to respond appropriately through the mind's preoccupation with the fearful emotion. The anxiety is fostered in the mind and the nervous system responds accordingly.

The gradual building of fear of public speaking is similar to Pavlov's famous behavioral experiment. Pavlov's dogs are well known for their seemingly inappropriate responses to the sound of a bell.

The experiment was quite simple. A bell was rung immediately before the dogs were fed. Over time, the dogs salivated at the sound of the bell whether there was food present or not. Their natural bodily responses were transferred to the sound of the bell.

Associations can be quite powerful. The mind can make an experience far worse than it really is. It is important to remember that you can control your thoughts and feelings to some extent. You can also retrain your body to have different responses to the experience of speaking in public.

UNLEARNING YOUR FEAR

The benefit of making associations thorough learned responses to stimuli is that these responses can be unlearned. The process does take some time but it is well worth the effort. There is more than one way to address the issue of relearning responses to various situations and objects.

A wonderful technique is to take a cognitive approach to addressing your public speaking fears. This is an effective way of using logic and rational thought in a deliberate manner. It may take some time to get accustomed to dealing with emotions on a cognitive level but it is a very viable tool once you have created an effective cognitive approach.

You can also retrain your responses on a behavioral level. Specialists who work in the field of behavioral psychology may refer to this as operant conditioning with a positive spin. If a negative experience can produce feelings of anxiety positive ones can create feelings of pleasure.

It is important to keep in mind that the fear of public speaking is one that is not based in an actual threat to your safety. It is a very common condition that is pretty universal in nature. You can opt to take your feelings of fear and anxiety and turn them into feelings of exhilaration and excitement.

LEARNED FEARS CAN BE UNLEARNED

People commonly navigate through their lives with a set of beliefs. Some of the beliefs are deeply rooted in fact. Some are products of faith. Others are based on an invalid perspective.

The fear of public speaking is frequently rooted in an irrational perspective. You may feel excessive anxiety and dread but there is realistically no basis for these feelings. Many people learn to be afraid to speak in front of a group through their experiences and their perception of the situation.

One obstacle people face is their perception of the audience. The group of people really poses no threat but the individual has taught himself that it does. Since the nervous system has been trained to respond with the physiological responses appropriate to fear the mind and body concur that the situation is one of danger.

Consider that a single traumatic event can lead to a lifetime of phobia and fear. The event may have lasted a mere second. It could have been observed rather than experienced first-hand. The lasting effect is evidence that we can revert back to a fearless response with practice. If one event can be so powerful several positive ones can be just as effective, if not more effective.

MIND OVER MATTER

We've all heard the "mind over matter" phrase at one time or another. This saying may be based in cognitive therapy. When a person takes a cognitive approach to a situation he addresses it with deliberate thought. Stepping away from emotions can be challenging but it can yield very good results.

Objectivity is not always easy especially when you are in the throes of emotion. The cognitive approach does take practice and it can be a little demanding but once you begin looking at public speaking objectively you begin to get control of the situation.

Feelings and thoughts are closely linked. You control your thoughts and you can use your thoughts to control your emotions over time. Following are some quick examples of using cognition to overcome your feelings of anxiety and fear about public speaking.

- Speaking in public is not inherently dangerous.
- You do not need to create a perfect presentation.
- Mistakes are a natural part of everyday life.
- The negative outcomes that you may fear are not realistic.
- The audience is not your enemy.
- You do not need to control every aspect of the presentation.

Each individual can cater his thoughts to his specific fears. Some may be afraid of different aspects of the presentation. You can decide which aspect of public speaking affects you the most and modify your thoughts appropriately.

RETRAINING YOUR RESPONSES

Just as you can retrain your thoughts you can also retrain your emotional responses to objects and situations. People are able to suppress fear reactions through desensitizing. This process is also known as exposure therapy.

Fear extinction is quite possible and there is a high rate of success among those who use processes like desensitizing and exposure therapy. Some believe that this approach works best if it is used intensely through a short period of time rather than stretching the process out over days or weeks.

FEAR EXTINCTION AND DESENSITIZING

Basically, exposure therapy and desensitizing help people in the process of fear extinction. They do this by replacing old memories with new ones. This approach may seem quite simple on the surface. Surprisingly, it is rather simple.

Fear memories are placed in the amygdala, a region of the brain. The process of controlling the emotion begins in the medial prefrontal cortex. This area of the brain sends messages to the amygdala and to the brain stem. The basic notion is that the brain's "safe" signal is also nestled in the amygdala.

People can be exposed to new experiences involving the source of fear. They can relearn how to react to the stimulus by retraining the brain. The frightful emotions housed in the amygadala can be replaced by feelings of safety. This carries into the brain stem where involuntary behaviors like heart rate and breathing are originated.

How is this simple? The process of making the magic work in the brain simply involves gradual exposure to the source of fear coupled with pleasant experiences. Those who want to overcome their fear of public speaking would expose themselves to the task in small doses and with great pleasure as the outcome.

The medial prefrontal cortex communicates the pleasantness of the experience to the amygadala and subsequently to the brain stem. These areas of the brain replace negative memories with pleasant ones and they help to control bodily fear responses.

Some suggest that this process should only take a few hours. Others suggest that the individual should practice exposing herself to public speaking over an extended period of time.

ALL ABOUT THE AUDIENCE

The audience is of the utmost importance when it comes to public speaking events. Your perception of the audience is the very cornerstone of your presentation. You can control how you view the crowd and you can quickly gain favor if you are empathetic.

This may seem difficult at first but after some consideration you will see that the audience is really your companion. The presentation is a two-way street in many cases. Some find great success through visualizing the audience as an alliance.

There are some examples of individuals who took their public speaking shortcomings and transformed them into impressive achievements. These individuals use the art and science of performing to overcome significant obstacles in their ability to articulate.

With inspiration on your side, you can opt to relinquish control of the situation to create a performance approach that works for you. Whether you want to create a public speaking persona or build a rapport with the audience for a single event, you can do so.

THE AUDIENCE WANTS YOU TO SUCCEED

Much of the anxiety that rests in the task of public speaking revolves around the speaker's perception of the audience. The fundamental fear can develop quite rapidly if the presenter sees the audience as a threat. You can do yourself a great favor by recognizing that the audience wants you to succeed.

Empathy is a big part of this general idea. Those sitting in the crowd are probably just as apprehensive about speaking in public as you are. They are well aware of what you are probably feeling and you may even use this to your advantage in your approach.

People are apt to enjoy someone who is confident. However, some humor and humility mixed into a presentation can do wonders. Public speaking in front of a live audience is interactive in nature. Just as a person is forgiving when you stammer across a sentence in one-on-one conversations, the crowd will be forgiving of your public speaking imperfections.

You may perceive a slip or a stammer to be a major obstacle but it really means very little to the audience. Consider that you will always judge yourself more harshly than anyone else. You are the biggest critic when it comes to your presentation.

Even if you imagine a handful of harsh critics in the audience, you can quickly overpower them. Consider someone saying, "Did you hear him pause at the inappropriate time?" Who is going to look like the fool? In the audience's eyes, it will be the critic because the majority of them know what it takes to speak in public.

MEETING EXPECTATIONS

Expectation is a complicated issue when it comes to the audience. Let's consider a person who really enjoys public speaking. This person may find the task to be so enjoyable because he knows that he needs to meet the audience's expectations.

Actors deliver lines. They are rehearsed, memorized and recited. The actor knows what to expect and he also has the benefit of a persona for delivery. When you look at the audience as having some expectations you may feel overwhelmed. However, these very expectations can help you overcome your fear.

Use the audience's expectations as a source of inspiration. Organize your information around what they want and need to know. Be empathetic. What would you expect a speaker to deliver? Would you shun this person for making a mistake?

INSPIRATION

Many people who are afraid of public speaking never dream of delving into the performing arts. However, there are many painfully shy individuals who do quite well in this field. There are some who use performance as a way to overcome articulation difficulties like stuttering and stammering.

One of the most outstanding examples is James Earl Jones. He stuttered and this prevented him from talking to others in social situations when he was a child. He overcame his articulation challenges by reading Shakespeare aloud to himself.

He did not use this approach until he was a high school student. His English teacher encouraged him to use this strategy. James Earl Jones managed to overcome his stutter and his shyness through reading aloud to himself, then to audiences. He later became one of the most recognized voices in Hollywood.

RELINQUISHING CONTROL

You may not be the next James Earl Jones but it is helpful to know that someone can overcome significant challenges if he puts his mind to it. Part of the challenge lies in control. Even though public speaking in front of a live audience is interactive in nature, it is necessary to relinquish control in order to overcome your fear.

People can feel much anxiety when others do not act they way they want them to. If some of the members of the audience seem distracted or fidgety they probably have their reasons. If some seem as if they are not paying attention, don't fret.

Your focus should be on the things you can control. Feed off of the people who are throwing positive energy in your direction. Some of the members of the audience may not respond as you would like. This is simply part of the process.

CREATING AN APPROACH

You can control your approach. A well thought-out strategy can do wonders for some speakers. Others may function better when they speak off the cuff. Too much rehearsal can backfire in some instances. Some people work well with notes. Some speakers have to dedicate the information to memory because the notes are too distracting.

Consider your own personality and think about how you naturally interact with others. If you are commonly relaxed and spontaneous, you might want to use a brief outline and speak naturally. If you like to plan things to the finest detail, you may want to include detailed notes. Only you can develop an approach that works for you.

Always remember the audience. Think about speeches and presentations that have impressed you in the past. You may choose to model after those events. This is a great strategy because you initially take the audience's point of view in this undertaking.

TIPS TO REMEMBER

There are great benefits to collecting a few tips about overcoming your fear of public speaking. These little threads of advice can help you use your resources well. The brevity of the tips is one of the most appealing aspects of the tidbits. They are easy to remember and you can even use small notebook for reminders and inspirations.

You will want to decide which tips will work best for you. Some of the suggestions will be of great interest to you while others may fall to the wayside. The purpose is to encourage you to take a first step into overcoming your fear of public speaking.

LETTING GO OF STRESS

Letting go of stress is much easier said than done and it always isn't realistic. It is important to keep in mind that stress can be a very good thing. Instead of fighting stress you can harness it to your benefit. This may be a new way of looking at stressful situations but it can yield wonderful results.

You have probably heard friends, relatives and associates tell you to let go of your stress. However, this approach doesn't work well for most of us. If it did, we would all be pretty much stress-free. Simply telling yourself to lose your stress can lead to feelings of anxiousness.

Stress, like fear, exists for a reason. The human body requires some stress in order to function properly. When pressure from this necessary component becomes overwhelming, it is necessary to use anxiety management techniques to help control the burdensome feelings.

Managing stress does not entail letting go of it. This natural anxiety can be harnessed effectively during a presentation. The very release of stress can function as a highly creative force that drives you through your public speaking venture.

NERVOUS ENERGY

One tip to remember in this realm is to think of stress as nervous energy. You can harness this energy source to your benefit. Considering that the anxiety is yours you should take charge of the emotion. This is far more productive than worrying about taking command of factors that are out of your locus of control.

Your nervous energy can serve several purposes. It can help you create a public speaking persona and it can be used for effective delivery. For example, you can focus on vocalization, volume and pauses with the stress energy you harness from within.

Performance is a matter of transforming nervous energy into a productive force. Some people naturally do this when they take the stage. Others require practice and training to accomplish this task effectively.

Learn to harness stress rather than letting it go. It is far too valuable as a tool for effective delivery for you to simply release it with no purpose.

Takeaway:

- Stress serves a purpose
- Nervous energy can be harnessed
- Laughter is a form of stress release
- Concentrate on using stress rather than overcoming it
- Focus on what you can control

KNOW YOUR LIMITATIONS

We all have our limits. If you are aspiring to create a stellar presentation that is going to take the world by storm then you may want to evaluate your situation. Creating realistic limitations for yourself is a great way to approach a public speaking venture.

Remember that the audience is on your side. No one really wants to see another person struggle through a presentation. It is nearly as painful to watch as it is to experience first-hand. Part of knowing your limitation involves setting attainable objectives and goals.

The goals are particularly effective if you are working with exposure therapy or desensitizing program. You can create small objectives that lead to larger goals. Breaking down the task into small, learnable steps is an effective approach to learning anything new.

And you are learning quite a few new things in this process. Not only are you unlearning your fear, you are replacing it with new experiences and emotions. You are learning the basics of oral presentation and you are learning how to harness nervous energy to your benefit.

The long list of learning in this process is more realistically achieved in smaller, doable steps rather than all at once. The last thing you want to do is jump into a vast public speaking engagement full force. Your limitations should be kept in check.

Takeaway:

- Lofty goals can work against your efforts
- Set realistic goals and objectives for yourself
- Break down the task of speaking in public into small steps
- You can always create larger goals as you progress

DO NOT OVER-PREPARE

Preparation for any oral presentation is a must for the average public speaker. Some naturally talented individuals can roll hours and hours of witty monologues off the cuff. You do not have to be Robin Williams in order to effectively speak in public.

There is no need to prepare to exhaustion and the very process of rehearsing to excess can work against you. Things rarely go smoothly. A person may distract you. It is easy to briefly lose your train of thought. Laughter may emerge out of the audience for no apparent reason.

This is simply part of speaking in front of a live audience. When you work to excess to prepare for an oral presentation you can be doing yourself a disservice. This falls back on to your locus of control. When you rehearse to excess you will probably buckle at the unexpected.

Preparing to excess can also lead to problems if you are really trying too hard. It is easy to become over zealous in your approach. You may try to squeeze too much information into a relatively small period of time. You can also be completely unprepared for spontaneous moments.

Takeaway:

- Rehearse effectively but not in excess
- If you feel that you are obsessing then you are probably over-preparing
- Prepare yourself for spontaneous moments
- Avoid packing too much information into one presentation
- Rote memorization is the lowest form of cognitive learning

PUBLIC SPEAKING TECHNIQUES THAT WORK

HUMOR

Laughter is a form of stress release. Keep in mind that your audience is under some stress during the presentation as well. You are in this together and one of the best approaches to creating a warm, welcoming atmosphere is to integrate humor into the mix.

You do not have to come up with knock-out one liners or delve into a book of jokes. Humor is most effective when you harness your nervous energy during your delivery. You can either create a public speaking persona or you can be your honest self in your delivery. Either way, a lighthearted approach can work wonders.

There are some obstacles to trying too hard to be humorous. Comedy requires a masterful sense of timing. Avoid trying to create a comedy routine. Just make the presentation warm, friendly and full of energy. Remember that you can not control every aspect of the audience's response. Laughter is not always what you seek.

The key to taking a humorous approach is to focus on making yourself and your audience comfortable. This involves smiling, eye contact (if possible) and an overall outpouring of well harnessed nervous energy. Think of being humorous as being personable.

When you address the audience as a warm, humorous person you help to create a win-win situation for you, your presentation and your audience. There are various elements that naturally occur to just about every public speaker that may seem to work against him. However, these very obstacles can be used in your favor as well.

SILENT MOMENTS

The silent pause is a great source of anxiety for many public speakers but it doesn't have to be. In fact, a pregnant pause can work wonders for a presentation if it is well placed. These moments can give your audience time to reflect on the information you are presenting and it can provide time for you to prepare for your next step.

Not all pauses are well planned. Some occur quite by accident. Some speakers may become further paralyzed with fear as they try to overcome their unnecessary pause. The silent moment can either work for you or against you. The choice is up to you.

A quick way around this potentially awkward moment is to simply repeat your last statement with emphasis and continue on. You can inject a little humor in the process or you can simply move forward as if the silence was planned.

It helps to remember that nothing bad is going to happen. If you perceive a silent moment, heckles or harsh questioning as an opportunity to move forward, you can create a win-win situation for yourself every time. Look at obstacles as opportunity.

MISTAKES

Mistakes are part of being a warm, humorous presenter. No one likes a robot that does everything to perfection. Your flaws can be your greatest assets. Your audience can relate to you much better if you are a little flawed even in your presentation.

For example, imagine being in the audience when a presenter asks for a moment to gather his thoughts. "I apologize. I just need a moment," she says. She takes a deep breath and opens to the audience with a genuine smile and an even more genuine, "Thank you." This is actually an effective opening that may have been planned from the start.

As long as you are honest, warm and welcoming in your presentation your mistakes will have little effect. In fact, they can work in your favor, especially if you can inject some well-timed humor into the mix. If not, no worries. Humility can work just as well as humor.

HUMILITY

There is something universally appealing about humility. An audience loves to relate to the speaker on some level. Pious, pretentious personas do not create a feeling of warmth and compassion. It may seem as if the suggestion is to "be yourself" but it is not.

You can create a persona to do your public speaking for you. It isn't necessary to hide your fear but it isn't necessary to put yourself out there on a personal level. Many public speakers develop a presenter personality that they use for their oral presentations.

This can be very effective if you are extremely knowledgeable about a certain subject. Your persona can help you discuss the topic on a personable level. This works much better than a cold lecture from an all-knowing, mistake-free presenter.

SPEAKING WITH PURPOSE

The purpose of your presentation is the driving force behind your performance. If you find the information tiresome and irritating it will come through in your delivery unless you are a very good actor. You can make nearly every subject interesting if you realize a notable purpose.

Look for the value in your message. Speakers are too often caught up in their anticipation of the experience, their fears and how others perceive them. If you consider the purpose, the value, of the speech above and beyond all else these issues fall to the wayside.

Having purpose will help you create a meaningful presentation that is driven by passion, not by fear. Speaking with the intent to influence, inform or entertain is not always enough. It helps to find value in your presentation. This can be difficult in some cases.

For example, you may find little value in overseeing a mandatory meeting at work. However, the meeting is mandatory for some reason. Find the reason. Create value and speak with purpose.

KEY POINTS

You may be surprised that a little information can go a very long way. In most situations you only need three or main points supported by evidence or anecdotal fillers. Memory aids are wonderful to use as well.

Consider that people rarely have total recall of a public speaking event. Auditory processing is quite complex and too much information can be overwhelming. Keep your information concise and in tune with purpose. This can be achieved by choosing three or four main points or fewer.

Too much information, too many facts and burdensome details can wreak havoc on your presentation. This works in a couple ways. Your audience may be confused about your core message and your purpose. They need to try and sort through what is and what is not important.

You are also causing yourself undo stress by trying to jam too much into one speech. Give yourself room and remember that your audience requires time to process the information. Emphasizing the same key points throughout the presentation will help your audience remember and it will help you stay focused.

Let's be brief about brevity. You have probably heard that brevity is the soul of wit. This stands true. Clear, concise language can do wonders for a presentation. Your audience will walk away with much more if you keep your information focused.

Well planned pauses, inflection and emphasis can help you create a brief delivery that has much more to offer than a boring lecture. You control the key points and you have the ability to help your audience recognize and retain them.

SELF PERCEPTION

Your self perception is of the utmost importance. Don't think of yourself as a public speaker. Why compare yourself to other presenters? You can develop your own style whether you are being yourself or whether you are using a public speaking persona.

There is no need to feel as if you have to be a professional speaker in order to do well. All you really need is to consider the audience, your message and the most effective way that you can deliver that message. Thinking of your self as a public speaker may lead to ridiculous expectations and feelings of inadequacy.

You really want to make the presentation about the purpose rather than about yourself. Worrying about how others perceive you is a waste of time. This is beyond the locus of your control. See yourself as a messenger with a purpose. This perception can take you a long way.

HELP AND SUPPORT

Support from others is a crucial factor in succeeding in your efforts to overcome your fear of public speaking. There are a number of different avenues to explore in the realm of support. Friends and family can offer much and there are groups that are designed to help people who share the same anxiety and fear as you do.

Consider the various resources available to you. Some people find relief through hypnosis. Others prefer to join a Toastmasters group. Public speaking classes can be very beneficial. Many are perfectly happy working with friends and family to practice and hone their skills.

FRIENDS AND FAMILY

Practicing in front of close friends and family is a wonderful way to introduce your self to the task of public speaking. You can gradually expose yourself to being in front of a crowd in a very safe, controlled environment. After some practice you may become much more comfortable in the role of the presenter.

This is a fundamental of exposure therapy and desensitizing. You know that you are safe. You will not be judged and the practice will be a pleasurable experience. It is important to remember that things do not have to go perfectly.

Choose your audience wisely. Hopefully, you will have a handful of friends and family that is willing to give you honest feedback. They should show a genuine interest in your success. This is a great opportunity to find out if you are speaking with purpose. The feedback should include your main points.

PUBLIC SPEAKING CLASSES

The notion of taking a public speaking class may not seem very appealing. You may prefer to give yourself a root canal. However, most people who take these classes share the same anxiety and fear as you do. There are many benefits to taking courses of this type.

The classes offer helpful techniques that are designed to help you deliver effective speeches. These tips and tricks can also help you improve your confidence. They can also help you overcome your fear.

Concentrating on purpose, style and technique rather than how others may perceive you is a fantastic approach to public speaking. Those who teach these classes can offer you a systematic method of learning which strategies will work for you. This also serves to help you take a cognitive approach rather than an emotional one.

HYPNOSIS

Hypnosis is another valuable tool for you to consider. Your fears are rooted in your thought processes and your body's physical reactions to fearful situations. Hypnosis can be considered a short cut in the process of overcoming the fear of public speaking.

Hypnosis is not necessary for everyone. A qualified health care provider should be your guide in this process. Common techniques used by the professional include visualization and relaxation. This approach is ideal for someone who has difficulty letting go of his fear.

TOASTMASTERS INTERNATIONAL

Toastmasters International is perhaps the most valuable resource available to you in your endeavor to overcome your fear of public speaking. This organization offers a vast array of services and support designed specifically for that task of helping others overcome their fears.

This organization offers a wealth of information and resources that are specific to your needs. Anyone who has a fear of public speaking can benefit from Toastmasters International. Even those who do not share the same fear can benefit from the information and resources offered by this outstanding organization.

Information ranges from basic tips and tricks to help you overcome your fears to inspirational stories. There is a great sense of comradely and belonging. Toastmasters International can offer something for people of all different levels of ability.

You can find an organization close to your place of residence for services and support. You may even feel inspired to start a club of your own through this resource after you have mastered the art of public speaking.

PUTTING IT ALL TOGETHER

Knowing the basics of the fear of public speaking can help you overcome the overwhelming anxiety associated with it. It is important to determine how severe your personal condition is when it comes to this fear. Once you have a grasp on you individual state you can begin to take steps.

Evaluating your specific needs is an important component to your success. You may find that a cognitive approach will work wonders for you or you may need to go as far as to seek professional help through a physician or hypnotist.

Remember that you are not alone in this fear. Many people share the same emotional and physical responses as you do. There are many reasons that you should keep this in mind when dealing with your public speaking fears. There are also many inspirational stories for encouragement.

Finally, you can opt to put theories into practice. Practical application of various techniques and approaches can help you work through your fears. Knowing how to overcome you fear of public speaking is not enough. You also need to develop a personal approach that works for you.

Fear is an important, natural response to various objects and situations. This essential emotion is valuable for self preservation. It may seem as if being afraid to speak in public is invalid. However, the primary notion of facing a crowd while standing alone makes the inherent nature of this fear very reasonable.

A phobia is an unreasonable, disabling fear that prevents a person from engaging in normal activities. In some instances, the phobia of public speaking (also known as glossophobia) may be the culprit behind a person's overwhelming fears.

ESTABLISHING YOUR PERSONAL STATE

Fear is such an inherently powerful emotion that it may be difficult to determine whether you are suffering from mere stage fright or whether you are experiencing glossophobia. There are considerations that you can make to determine how severe your condition really is.

If you are unable to function normally on a day-to-day basis because of the remote possibility that you may have to speak in public then you might want to consult a professional. A phobia can be treated very effectively and you may be surprised by how effective treatment can be.

Everyone has different needs our memories and experiences are unique and the severity of our fears can vary greatly. Try taking small steps by visualizing yourself speaking in front of a small audience. Does it seem plausible or do you feel an overwhelming sense of dread?

You may find that hypnosis or professional therapy is in order. Some go as far as to use medications in more severe cases. Some medicines can inhibit fear responses, helping the person deal with the situation more effectively.

Others find that taking a cognitive approach that helps them view the public speaking engagement on a rational rather than emotional level work wonders. You may find that working in collaboration with classmates in a public speaking class offers the greatest benefits or you may find help with a close-knit group of family and friends.

Toastmasters International is an ideal resource for help and inspiration for nearly everyone who has a fear of speaking in public. This organization is dedicated to helping people in overcoming this specific fear.

A UNIVERSAL PROBLEM

A brave person is not a fearless person. What makes the individual brave is his ability to overcome his fears. Few people are immune to the fear of public speaking. This is a natural feeling that is worthy of recognition. Your effort to take control of your fear is the fundamental element of true bravery.

The physical and psychological responses to speaking in front of a crowd are perfectly natural. They just vary greatly from person to person. The dry mouth, shaking and shortness of breath are to be expected at some level. You can work to use these responses in a positive way.

All of the natural bodily responses can be considered forces of energy. You can harness that energy into a positive force that is used in your delivery. Your nervous energy can be your best friend.

THE AUDIENCE IS ON YOUR SIDE

Since the fear of public speaking is somewhat inherit, it is easy to understand that you face a sympathetic audience each and every time. Nearly everyone can relate to your fear. Instead of viewing the audience as an obstacle, it helps to view the crowd as an alliance.

The audience is there for a reason. There is a valid purpose for your presentation. Once you focus your energy on the audience's needs and your purpose your fears will fall to the wayside.

Offering humility and humor in your presentation is another great approach to working with an audience. Recognize that the group shares your fears and they respect your bravery. There is great benefit to re-seeing the audience in your presentation.

Your self perception is a powerful tool as well. Those who try to approach public speaking with the notion that they have to be outrageously talented, smart and witty will most likely be overwhelmed. Consider yourself as an individual with a purpose.

There is energy flowing between the speaker and the audience. You can use the very things that make you nervous to work in your favor. It is helpful to recognize that you and the audience are in this together.

CONCLUSION

One way to overcome this emotion is to re-establish your self perception. Do not view yourself as a public speaker facing a crowd. Consider yourself as an integral part of the audience. You are an extension of the insight and information that the audience needs and wants.

Overcoming any fear takes practice. Different levels of severity require different types of approaches. Each person is an individual with unique experiences and associations. It is best to cater an approach that works for you.

PRACTICAL APPLICATION

Simply knowing something is not enough. Storing information in the back of your brain yields little results. It takes effort to put theory into practice. Once you have decided which approaches to try, it is necessary to put forth the effort.

Practical application of what you have learned can begin with something as simple as visualizing yourself giving a speech in public. The audience can be any size you choose. This step is ideal for someone who doesn't really know whether he has a fear or a phobia.

USING YOUR KNOWLEDGE

Your knowledge base should help you re-see the situation. You are no longer the public speaker. The expectations are realistic and you are able to take an objective, cognitive approach to the task. This requires practice. Thinking past your emotional responses is an art in itself that requires mastery.

Hone your skills by creating a small speech that contains a single main idea. Are you able to drive the point through with purpose? Do you feel the need to speak during each and every second of the presentation? Step back and evaluate your progress.

Taking an objective approach to a fearful situation may require you to delve into the origin of your fear. Consider how the brain is automatically wired for certain responses and your nervous system makes your body react in kind. Are you able to look at these responses objectively?

USING YOUR RESOURCES

One of the best things you can do to take steps to overcoming your fear is to delve into the resources available to you. The primary resource is Toastmasters International. This organization offers a vast wealth of information and there is a great sense of belonging in these groups.

Friends, family and trusted associates can offer support. It helps to make sure that these resources are open and honest in their reactions. You can get to the core of your fear by practicing in a safe environment surrounded by people who are genuinely invested in your success.

If you believe that your fear borders on glossophobia then you may want to speak with a professional. There are resources available that can help you work through the phobia including desensitizing and exposure therapy. Some severe cases may require medication.

Hypnosis is an appealing solution for many individuals. This approach is particularly helpful for those interested in retraining the brain to respond to the public speaking environment differently. Hypnosis can be seen as a sort of shortcut to extinction.

TAKING STEPS TO OVERCOME YOUR FEAR

A plan of action is required in order for you to progress. Consider James Earl Jones and his speech impediment. He used something that was of great interest to him to turn his weakness into one of his greatest strengths. The process of overcoming the stutter required considerable, dedicated action on his part.

Use your passions to overcome your fear. If you feel strongly about a certain topic, begin practicing through this subject. Keep your subject within your interests at first. Later, you will be able to create presentations that have purpose and interest no matter what subject matter.

THOUGHTFUL PRACTICE

Practice comes in many forms. You may want to recite your favorite poem aloud in a secluded place. Perhaps you have a presentation related to your profession already planned. No matter what, you want to focus on the message instead of your delivery.

Thoughtful practice involves a deliberate use of nervous energy. You can use your anxiety in positive ways. Practicing with deliberate thought combined with effective relaxation techniques will yield excellent results.

RELAXATION TECHNIQUES

You do need some stress especially when it comes to delivering a speech. How the stress affects you is the primary concern. Relaxation techniques are quite personal and they differ from individual to individual. Your specific approach should be designed to create a balance between your anxiety and your effective delivery.

Traditional approaches include picturing the audience naked. This does little more than trivialize the group. It is probably better to create a visualization of the audience as a group of people in need of information. You are merely there to deliver the message effectively.

Becoming familiar with the process is a very important aspect of your success. The old adage "practice makes perfect" holds true in the realm of public speaking. Using your knowledge base and your resources can take you very far in your endeavor.

Consider the first time you tried any task. There are times when the task was completed with seemingly effortless ease. Other times you struggled over and over again to achieve success. You did master the tasks in most cases whether they required great effort of whether they were simple for you to learn.

It is important to remember that the outcome is the same for each situation. You can overcome your fear of public speaking. The only difference between you and a naturally talented speaker is the time it takes to reach the goal.

UNIT 4: 100 Public Speaking Tips

Before we end, here are 100 tips for you to remember and practice.

1. Build your confidence.

One of the keys to effective public speaking is to become more confident. You have to believe that you are good in what you do; and, in order to achieve that, you need to be prepared by properly researching about the topic you are going to talk about. Aside from that, better confidence can also come from more practice.

2. Look at yourself on the mirror.

If you want to improve your public speaking skills, then you should practice in front of the mirror. By doing this, you would be able to see how you look like while doing your stuff. With that, you can see whether you need to improve your stance, the way you open your mouth, the expression of your eyes, and such.

3. Listen to yourself.

Practicing public speaking can go a long way, as far as giving your audience a pleasant experience in listening and watching you in front. However, you should also listen to your voice. Practicing your speech countless times can help. But, it would be better if you can record your voice, and listen to it, so that you can really hear how your voice sounds to your audience.

4. Practice your memorization skills.

Sharpening your mind can help you with public speaking. This is because, in most cases, when you have to present something in front of an audience, you have prepared a script for it.

Improving your memorization skills can be done by playing more mind games, or by simply reading books and trying to memorize a few paragraphs in it.

5. Improve your looks.

Always keep in mind that when you speak in public, people would be looking at you. Although most people would not care much about what you wear, or how you are wearing your hair while speaking in front, it is still best to make it a point to look at your best. By wearing something that you know you would look good in, you would become more confident, which can give you a good start in speaking.

6. Learn more about public speaking.

Researching about different techniques or tricks about public speaking can help you improve your skills on it. Doing your research can be done by reading more books and magazines about it. Aside from visiting bookstores for them, you can also check out websites, which may offer eBooks about public speaking or are offering valuable information for free.

7. Seeking more help in public speaking.

Hiring someone to help you with public speaking can also be a good step to take, towards gaining success in it. However, you need to make sure that the person you are hiring really has good experience when it comes to it. Aside from that, it is best that he is someone who has been recommended to you by your friends or relatives.

8. Start with a smaller audience.

If you think that facing a pretty large crowd can be quite overwhelming, then you should speak in front of a fewer number of people first. Get your family involved with it by asking them to be your first audience. You can also ask your friends to listen to you if you want to. When you practice, pretend that you don't know them, so that it would become more realistic.

9. Take care of your voice, especially days before speaking in public.

One of the keys to being effective in public speaking is to have a nice and clear voice. Thus, you should take care of it, especially just days before your presentation. That means, you should not have cold drinks, and you should also avoid staying out late at nights. Additionally, you should also refrain from shouting.

10. Modulate your voice.

Voice modulation simply means changing the pitches of your voice. Modulating your voice would prevent your audience to get bored or confused. Aside from that, with effective modulation, it can help you give more emphasis on certain words. Learn more about how moving your pitches up and down can affect your speech, so that you can put it to good use.

11. Give it time.

You should keep in mind that it can take some time to become a skilled presenter. Thus, you should practice more, and don't get easily discouraged if you are not as effective as you have expected yourself to be. Practice more, and aim higher, so that you can attain your goals soon.

12. Determination.

Being determined in whatever you do, can take you to places with it. Thus, you should be determined in providing your audience a presentation that they would truly remember. Your determination can help you in preparing for it. Aside from that, you should study well, and tailor the content of your speech to properly match with your audience.

13. Be persistent.

You cannot expect an overnight success in public speaking. If you want to become really good in it, you need to work hard for it, as well as spend time. Aside from that, you should also hone your skills by attending more trainings in public speaking. Moreover, you can also get it contact with an expert in the field, so that he can train you.

14. Become more passionate in your topic.

If you want the people in front of you to listen to what you have to say, then you should show them that you are very interested in it. Thus, you should take note of the subtopics that you really love, of the subject you would talk about, so that you can give more emphasis to them, while speaking. By doing that, you can show your audience that you are one of the persons to refer to when it comes to the topics you are talking about.

15. Let your audience know that you are a real person.

Whenever you want to tell your audience examples or situations to illustrate what you are trying to explain better, don't forget that your unfavorable experiences can also help. In doing this, you would let your audience see that you are indeed a real person. Aside from that, it can also help in making them see that you are sincere.

16. Grab your audience's attention.

One of the best ways to grab the attention of your audience is to tell a funny story. Aside from that, you can also cite an anecdote or a quotation for it. You want to do this at the first part of your presentation, so that people would listen to you. Once you have their attention, you can expect them to listen to all the important things you have to say.

17. The right way to prepare.

One of the keys to proper preparation for a presentation is to gather important information about your topic. Researching can now be done through the internet, which is more convenient. If you are able to uncover important materials for your topic though, once you are done with your speech, don't throw it away, since you may have good use for it in the future.

18. Tell stories.

While you are giving your piece, you want to tell stories related to it, so that people would continue listening to you. When you tell stories about other people though, make sure that you also get to know them well. This way, you can tell your audience about certain facts about such persons, which can make them realize that the stories are indeed true.

19. Don't just rely on your voice.

Keep in mind that people learn not just through listening in the lecture, but also through visual stimulation. Thus, aside from developing a good voice for it, you should also check your facial expressions. More importantly, don't forget that you can also make use of props, visual aids, and other tools that can help you captivate your audience.

20. Don't forget about time.

When you are going to give a presentation, don't forget about its allotted time. You don't want to have someone waving at you, and giving you signals that you are out of time, when you are still halfway through your speech. Thus, take note of the allotted time, and make your speech fit it appropriately.

21. Watch masters in public speaking more often.

Whether it would be through seminars or television, you should watch masters in public speaking more often. This way, you get to take note of their techniques, their habits, and other good practices. Watch them, so that you can also get a better idea on what makes them successful public speakers.

22. Check the room or the venue.
As much as possible, you want to visit the room or the venue that you are going to do your presentation on. This way, you would become more familiar with the environment where you are going to present in front of a group of people. If it is possible though, spend some time in the spot where you are going to speak, so that you can have an idea on what it would be like.

23. Know your audience.
Learning more about your audience can help you a lot when it comes to the kind of speech or presentation you want to have. For example, if you are going to present in front of professionals, then you should keep it formal, but don't forget to throw out some jokes. This can keep them from becoming bored.

24. Be sober.
It is never a good idea to drink some alcoholic beverages prior to giving out a speech. There are actually some people who believe that drinking a bottle of beer can help them gain more courage in facing a crowd. However, it is much better to listen to someone who is sober, even if he shows some signs of nervousness, than listening to someone who is drunk.

25. Learn as much as you can about the topic you are going to talk about.
Spend as much time as you can in researching about the topic you are going to talk about. This is to make sure that you are as prepared as you can, in giving your presentation. Keep in mind that the more prepared you are, that more effective you can be in delivering your speech. Thus, it can also boost your self-confidence, which is very important in public speaking.

26. Anticipate possible questions from your audience.

If the kind of presentation you are going to make would give an opportunity for some people to ask questions, then you should be prepared for it. One way of doing this is to anticipate possible questions from your audience, and preparing professional answers to them. Try to come up with the most difficult and unexpected questions, so that you won't be caught off guard when someone asks them.

27. Practice more.

The more you are going to practice your presentation, the more you would become an expert on it. Thus, you should practice more often. Practice in front of your kid, your spouse, your dog, as well as in front of the mirror. Time your presentation, and give more emphasis on those points that are more challenging.

28. Be comfortable.

The more comfortable you are in front, the more effective you can be in conveying your message. To achieve that, you should make sure that you are comfortable with what you are wearing. Aside from that, keep in mind that it can also be achieved when you have properly prepared for the speech.

29. Be positive.

When you constantly think of negative thoughts, then you may not become successful in public speaking. Thus, you should always think that you are great in it, so that you would be able to attain that. When you constantly have positive thoughts, you would become more confident in yourself, and have the motivation to constantly improve.

30. Giving your audience what they want.

It is best if you know what your audience want, before you have your presentation. This way, you would be able to convince them to listen to you all throughout your speech. Thus, if your audience what to be entertained, then you should not hesitate in telling a couple of funny stories, which are all related to the topic you are talking about.

31. Don't forget to bring some notes.

When you do your public speaking, it is necessary to have some notes in front of you, in order to have something as your guide, as far as following a certain flow in your speech. Thus, you should prepare them beforehand. Make the notes small, but highlight some words, so that you can easily see them at a glimpse.

32. Don't put yourself down.

Don't be too hard on yourself, if you feel that you have not given your presentation a hundred percent. Always remember that you can always make some adjustments on your upcoming presentations, so that you can improve further. Aside from that, it does not necessarily mean that your audience did not enjoy your speech, if you think that it was not good.

33. Public speaking is not a matter of life or death.

You should learn to relax when you are speaking in front of a crowd. When you miss out on something that you have on your notes, you should remember that no one except you would know that. Aside from that, no one is going to shout at you if you missed an image in your visual aids.

34. Don't tell your audience that you are nervous about your speech.

If you are nervous about your speech, it is actually not the best move to tell your audience about it. If you do, then they may see you as someone who lacks experience and better skills in public speaking. Thus, it is best to hide it, and gain control over it. Sound more confident at the beginning, and you will realize that just prior to hitting your first minute in front, all your nervousness would already be gone.

35. Give it your best shot.

Every time you speak in front of a crowd, make it a point to always give it your best shot. This means that you should always try to make it your best speech ever. By doing it this way, you are always challenging yourself to be better on it, and you are recognizing the fact that there is always room for improvement.

36. Don't speak too fast.

One of the most obvious signs of nervousness and lack of confidence is when a speaker begins to talk real fast. Thus, even if you are nervous, you should learn how to pace yourself. Always remember that when you talk fast, in most cases, your audience may not be able to understand what you are saying. Thus, slow down at bit, so that you can also gain more control over your nervousness.

37. Try to avoid looking at the eyes of the people in front of you.

If it is your first time to speak to a large crowd, then try to avoid looking at the eyes of people nearest to you, since it can make you more nervous. This does not mean that you should look at the floor, ceiling, or your sides. Always remember that they want you to look them in the eye; however, if you are too nervous in doing it, you should look at their forehead instead.

38. Take a deep breath.

If you are trembling, especially when you are just a few seconds away to being called for your speech, you should practice deep breathing. Taking a deep breath can help in calming your nerves. Thus, just before you position yourself in front of the crowd, take a deep breath, so that you would become more relaxed, and be rid of your nervousness.

39. Be funny, but don't overdo it.

Telling jokes that are related to the topic you are talking about can be an effective technique in getting your audience's attention. However, you should not over do it. When you tell too many jokes, some people may think that you are a comedian instead of a professional public speaker. Aside from that, it can also take away the validity of your presentation..

40. Everyone makes mistakes.

Making mistakes is actually normal. Thus, you should not worry too much about them. For example, if you mispronounced a couple of words, you should not dwell too much about it, since it can affect your whole presentation. What you need to do instead, is to acknowledge them, and to simply move forward.

41. Keep it short and simple.

Always remember that not too many people love to hear or watch long speeches and presentations. Thus, you should keep it short and simple, as much as you can.

However, make sure that you are able to cover all the important topics, so that your audience are able to gather important information from your speech.

42. View yourself as the messenger.

It is highly unlikely that you would be asked to give a presentation about yourself or your life story. Thus, always keep in mind that your presentation is not about you. It is actually about the topic that you are going to talk about. With that, view yourself as the messenger that would convey the information to the audience, so that you can focus more on that, instead of focusing on yourself.

43. Try to fake it.

If you don't have confidence on yourself when it comes to public speaking, then you should fake it. Faking it means that you should try to act that you are confident, when you are in front and talking to your audience. By doing that, they would listen to you more attentively, and eventually, you would even gain the confidence you didn't have.

44. Just be yourself.

Watching experts in the field of public speaking can help you in a lot of ways, but it is best not to mimic them. This is because, some people in the audience may be familiar of the techniques and styles that you are copying. Just pick some good points from the experts, and be yourself, so that you would be able to come up with your own style that people would love.

45. Practice yoga.

Yoga does not only provide you relief from stress, but it can also maintain the health of your voice and your throat. Thus, you should practice yoga more often. By performing certain yoga techniques, you would be able to clear your throat, and prevent all sorts of problems that are related to your voice.

46. Always remember that your audience is the most important part of your presentation.

Don't forget that every time you have a presentation, it is not for yourself, but for your audience. Thus, you should keep in mind that they are the most important part of your presentation. With that, make sure that you are able to deliver a speech that can catch their attention, so that they would be able to benefit from it.

47. Say what the audience want to hear.

Saying what you want can help you become more comfortable in speaking in front.

However, if you want your presentation to become more effective, then say things that your audience need to hear. Always remember that people are listening to you, because they are hoping to learn from your presentation. Thus, you should focus more on what they need, so that you can come up with an effective speech.

48. What to do, when you are called for an impromptu speech.
If your employers have called you for an impromptu speech, there are certain things to do, to make it your best. One of which is to immediately stand, and avoid showing any kind of hesitation, so that you will gain a more commanding presence. Aside from that, keep in mind that your bosses would not have requested you for the presentation, if they believe that you are not ready for it.

49. What to do when some people are not listening.
When someone is not listening to you, one of the things that you can do is to increase the volume of your voice a bit. Aside from that, you should also try to make eye contact with them, in order to grab their attention. By doing that, you are actually giving them signals that you noticed that they are not listening.

50. Arrive at the venue early.
When you arrive late at the venue where you are going to do your presentation, you may not be able to prepare yourself properly for it. Thus, it is best if you can be at the place at least 30 minutes either before your speech, or even before the program starts. By doing that, you can do all the necessary preparations you need, in order to feel more comfortable and be at ease at the place.

51. Being nervous is normal.
Don't be too worried about being nervous, since it is perfectly normal. In fact, even some of the most experienced public

speakers still feel their legs trembling, prior to giving their speeches. What makes them look like they do not fear being in front of people is their confidence. When you are confident, you will be able to overcome your nervousness, and become more comfortable in the latter part of your speech.

52. Don't let certain things distract you.

When you are speaking in front of a large crowd, there is always a possibility for certain things to distract you. Some of which would include certain individuals standing up while you are talking, or late comers opening the doors. Keep in mind that these things will only become your distractions if you let them.

53. Preventing people from looking outside the windows.

If your presentation is going to be at a small room, where a certain number of participants are seated in front of you, you don't want them to constantly look outside the windows and miss out important points from your speech. To prevent this, you can make sure to close the blinds just before starting your piece. Aside from preventing people looking outside, you can also minimize distractions by not having to see other individuals looking from outside.

54. Sort out any problems beforehand.

Whenever there are problems in the venue, it is best if you sort them days before the event. Thus, it is best if you can visit the venue to thoroughly check it days before your speech. If that is not possible, then be there an hour prior to the start of the program, so that you can fix any issues immediately.

55. Don't forget to check the sound system.

Speaking in front of a large crowd can be frustrating, if you know that some people seated at the back are not able to hear you well. Thus, make sure that the venue can offer a good sound system. Aside from having adequate volume, the sound should also be in good quality, so that people would be able to understand you perfectly.

56. Words you should always remember.

Some of the words you should always remember and tell yourself would include prepared, poised, powerful, persuasive, commanding, composed, and confident. When you do this, you would eventually feel that you can deliver a great speech. Aside from that, it can also make your audience see that you are a person that can be described by the words mentioned on top.

57. What not to do when unprepared.

If you have not been able to prepare yourself for the presentation, one of the things that you should not do is to apologize. This should not be done, since it will make you feel less confident. Aside from that, people may not want to listen to you, since they won't be expecting much from your presentation.

58. Take full advantage of your notepads or index cards.

There may be times when you get stuck on what sub topic you want to explain next. To prevent this from happening, you should take advantage of your index cards, and write down your opening phrases in bold letters on top of them. By doing that, you won't have to deal with a long pause, since you can simply read them out and continue from there.

59. Become more familiar of the visual equipment you would be using.

If you are simply going to borrow a projector or any kind of visual equipment at the venue, then you should familiarize yourself in operating it. You don't want to get your presentation delayed, just because you don't know how to turn to the next page, or to return back to a previous one. Therefore, spend some time with it prior to your presentation, so that you would know how to operate it perfectly.

60. Avoid technical jargons.

When your presentation is technical in nature, you may get tempted in using technical terms for it. However, you should consider the possibility that some of the people in your audience may not understand them. Thus, it is best to make use of simple terms, so that you can ensure that all of them would know what you are talking about.

61. When involved with a sales presentation.

If your presentation is about sales, then make sure that you make it as lively as possible, especially if you want to motivate your audience to making more sales. This is because, the energy in your presentation can determine the kind of motivation the sales force would have when they leave the room. Aside from that, you should also make sure that you tell them stories that can inspire them.

62. Don't worry about the few who may not appreciate your presentation.

After your presentation, you would know if people like it when they start clapping their hands, smile at you, or stand in ovation. However, you may notice that some would simple go out of the room, or are clearly not satisfied. When this happens, remind yourself that you cannot please them all. Thus, just let them go, and appreciate the fact that most of the individuals who listened to you are happy with what they learned.

63. A presentation is not the time to wear something new.

Trying out a new pair of shoes in a presentation may not be a very good idea. This is because, you still do not know, whether wearing it can still be comfortable even after standing for quite some time. This is also applicable to wearing a new shirt or a new pair of pants, since you want to be very comfortable during your speech.

64. How to project your voice properly.

Projecting your voice is essential in order to make sure that people can hear you clearly. Keep in mind though that voice projection is completely different from shouting. You need to make use of your diaphragm when you do it, so that it would sound good, and more commanding.

65. What to do when an error is committed.

When you said something wrong, or you made an error in using the visual aid, try not to apologize for it. Chances are, your audience may not have even noticed it. Thus, if you are going to apologize for it, then people listening to your speech would realize that you made a mistake. Some would probably take note of it; however, many would not even care, as long as you provide them with valuable information.

66. Using a whiteboard.

If you want to make use of a whiteboard for your presentation, make sure that the pens are working, prior to using them. This is because, visual aids are also very important, when it comes to helping people understand your message better. Aside from that, you don't want to delay your presentation by spending time in looking for a pen that actually works.

67. Learn more about PowerPoint.

PowerPoint is a program that can help you a lot when it comes to having an effective presentation. It is true that you can hire someone to make the PowerPoint presentation for you, in accordance to your report. However, it is best if you are the one who makes it, especially if it is quite long, so that you are more comfortable and effective in using it.

68. Using a script.

While it is true that you can come up with your own script for a presentation, it is not actually a good idea to use a full script for the whole part of it. This is because, it can make you sound boring. Aside from that, people can also notice that you lack in emotion. Thus, make a script for your presentation just for the purpose of having guide for it, so that people would appreciate it more.

69. Practice your entrance.

Arriving early at the venue where you are going to do your presentation can give you a chance to practice your entrance. Practicing your entrance can help in making you more comfortable in delivering your speech. Thus, try to practice getting on the stage when no one is around yet, so that you can gain more confidence.

70. The right way to end the presentation.

The last thing that you should do prior to ending your presentation is to deliver your "call to action" phrase. This should be done after the question and answer portion, as well as the part where you show your appreciation to the audience and organizers. By doing that, your "call to action" phrase would remain in the minds of the participants, once they leave the venue.

71. How to make sure your voice is loud enough.

If you are unsure whether people at the back can hear you, then one way around it is to have a friend stand or sit at that part of the venue. By doing that, he can give you signals that would indicate whether your voice is loud enough or not. Just make sure that you agree on the signals, so that you won't get confused.

72. Check your slides prior to the presentation.
When people have not arrived at the venue yet, try to sit at the back of the venue, after turning on the slides. This would give you an opportunity to check whether people sitting at the back rows would be able to see your slides properly. With that, it can still give you time to make adjustments when needed.

73. Don't rely on your slides too much.
Some people think that with their slides, they would have something to refer to when it comes to reminding themselves what to talk about next. Keep in mind that your audience can also read the slides, which can make them get ahead of you. Aside from that, if the slides won't work, then you may not know what to talk about next. Thus, it is best to practice your presentation without the slides, and carry some notes about it during the presentation.

74. Turn off your phone prior to your speech.
Turning off your mobile phone prior to your speech can help you focus more on the task at hand. Aside from that, it can also help in preventing you from getting distracted with unimportant text messages. Some people think that putting the phone in silent mode would also suffice. However, when in silent, you may have programmed it to vibrate, which can still become a distraction.

75. Know why your audience come to your presentation.
When you are able to identify the possible reasons why your audience have come to your presentation, then the better your presentation becomes. This is because, you would be able to tailor your presentation in accordance to their reasons. Do your research, so that you can ensure that they would appreciate your presentation more.

76. Stop or minimize using word fillers.

There may be times when you use lots of errs and ums in your speech, which is not good to hear. To put a stop to it, then you may ask your friend for assistance. A friend can help you by standing at the back, and raising his hand each time you use word fillers, to remind you not to do it again.

77. What to take note of, when presenting in front of a small group.

If you are presenting in front of a smaller sized group, then most likely, they are decision makers of big companies. Thus, you need to do thorough and formal in giving your presentation. Aside from that, make sure that you know each one of them, as well as their interests in your presentation, prior to starting it.

78. Looking at the eye of a person.

It is a good idea to look at the person in the eye, when you deliver a phrase in your presentation. This is because, it can create an effect that you are sincere in it, and are confident. However, when you continue with the next phrase, you should look at another person for it, so that the other one won't get uncomfortable.

79. Summarize your speech.

Just before ending your speech, it is best to summarize it, so that people would be able to get your message more effectively. When you come up with your summary, you should focus on the purpose of your speech. Thus, you should determine whether it would be to persuade, entertain, or to provide important information.

80. Keep the facts coming.

Always remember that in most cases, people are watching your presentation, in order to learn more from it. Thus, you should focus on providing more facts to your audience. These facts should be derived from credible sources, and you should double check if they are accurate and true.

81. Take note of your gestures, movements, and facial expressions.

Your gestures, movements, and facial expressions can give your audience an idea about a lot of things about you. By watching them, your audience would know whether you are confident in your speech or not, as well as how well you know your topic. Thus, make sure to take note of them, so that you can have your audience see you as a professional speaker, who is an expert on his topic.

82. Remember the add-ons to speeches.

Three add-ons you want to take note of would include handouts, humor, and audiovisual aids. Handouts can help your audience in taking note of the topics that you are about to talk about. On the other hand, humor can make them enjoy your presentation. Lastly, the audio-visual aids would ensure that they are able to understand your topic fully.

83. Use gestures to complement your words.

When there are words that you want to emphasize more, you should make use of gestures for it. For example, if you are talking about a big cat, then show it to them with the use of your arms. Doing it this way would not just help your audience understand you better, but it can also catch their attention.

84. Conducting a Q and A portion of the presentation.

Not every presentation may not provide you a chance to have a question and answer portion. However, if you are given a chance to have one, then you should take advantage of it. The Q and A portion of the speech would not just help you convey your message more effectively, but it can also make the impression that you are not just a speaker, but also an expert.

85. Expect the unexpected.

When you are expecting the unexpected, it does not necessarily mean that you are thinking negatively. It simply means to be prepared for it. Thus, you should be prepared on what to do, just in case the lights would go out, or the projector is not working, so that you would be able to take action for it immediately.

86. Aim for continuous improvement.

You should always remember that no presentation or speaker is perfect. Thus, you should always aim to make improvements. One way to achieve that is to seek feedback. The feedback does not have to come from experts in the field. You can also solicit it from people, especially those who are part of your audience.

87. Study other speakers.

Checking out other speakers by joining conferences and seminars is a good way to improve your public speaking skills. When you listen to them, try to study their strengths and weaknesses, and compare their styles with one another. By doing that, it can help you improve on your strengths more, and overcome your weaknesses.

88. Don't forget to share your personal experiences.

Sharing your personal experiences in your speech is a good idea to captivate your audience. Just make sure that you are going to tell them an experience of yours, which is related to your topic. When you tell them a real story, which involves you in it, then they would listen to everything that you say, and see you as a real person.

89. Overcoming stage fright.

You would know that you have stage fright when you start to sweat excessively, have dried up lips and mouth, and trembling knees. When you experience it just before you are to deliver your speech, it does not necessarily mean that you need to back out. There are lots of things that you can do to overcome it; and, one of which is to think that most of the people you are going to speak to do not have a good background on your topic.

90. Don't eat a few minutes before your speech.

If you want to have good energy when you speak to your audience, then you should not eat just a few minutes before you begin. In fact, it is best to eat 3 hours before your speech, so that your body is almost done processing the food you have eaten. This means that it is already utilizing it, in order to perk up your body for your presentation.

91. Sleep well.

The night before your public speaking event, you should make sure to get at least 8 hours of sleep. This way, you would have the energy that you need, in order to prepare and deliver your piece. Without enough rest, aside from not having enough energy to deliver a good speech, you may even have the tendency to forget certain parts or details of your presentation.

92. Drink adequate amounts of water.

Hours before your presentation, you should drink lots of water, and taper it down, as you go nearer to the time when you are called by the facilitator to be in front. This is to make sure that your mouth and throat won't get dried out. Aside from that, you want to taper it down, so that you won't feel like going to the comfort room while delivering your presentation.

93. Eat the right kinds of foods.

You need to become more familiar of the foods that can upset your stomach, if you want to be in top condition for your presentation. This way, you would be able to avoid them days before the event, and, especially on the day of the event. Upsetting your stomach on your speech day is not a good idea, since you can get distracted by your urge to go to the comfort room.

94. Work out.

Working out weeks before your presentation can actually provide you with benefits for it. When you work out, you will be able to have lots of energy when public speaking day arrives. Aside from that, it can also boost your confidence, especially since you know that you look and feel fit.

95. Do not expect achieving excellence on your first try.

If it is your first time to do public speaking, chances are, you may be able to do good at it, but it may not be your best yet. This is because public speaking is actually a skill, which you need to learn and master in time. Thus, you need to do all the necessary preparation for your first try, be relaxed in delivering your piece, and know that you can make improvements on it the next time.

96. Have public speaking style that suits your personality.

There are lots of different public speaking styles that you can use on stage. However, you should use a style that suits your personality, in order to be effective on it. Some of the styles would include laid back and casual, humorous and fast paced, and a lot more.

There is no need to follow a particular style to the letter. Just be yourself, and you will soon be able to come up with your own style.

97. Establish your presence right at the beginning of your speech.

In order to grab the attention of your audience, you need to establish your stage presence right at the beginning of your presentation. This can be done by starting strong, and showing them that you are confident. Aside from that, you can also tell them a joke or two, as long as you don't stray far from your topic.

98. Repeat the question.

If you are having a question and answer portion, then always remember to repeat the question. Repeating or paraphrasing the question can help to ensure that you understand it perfectly. Aside from that, it can also ensure that other members of the audience would know what the question is all about.

99. Wear clothes in accordance to the venue.

Keep in mind that there are venues that can be cold, while others may be a bit warm. Therefore, it is best that you know the kind of temperature you could experience from the venue you are having your presentation. This way, you can wear something that would be appropriate for it, so that you would feel more comfortable.

100. Smile throughout your speech.

Smile is something that is contagious; and, you can use it while delivering your speech, so that you can encourage a more positive atmosphere. Aside from that, when you smile while you are making your presentation, you would also feel at ease. Moreover, people would also be encouraged to listen to you, when they see you smiling.

* * * * *

9 788819 463343